Follow Me
Daring to Live the Life of Full Abandon

Ryan Bash

To Cameron and Cailynn
That you might desire nothing but life in the presence of Jesus

Teleios Press

Printed in the United States of America

First edition 2013

TELEIOS PRESS

Foreword

I like guys who can speak well, write well, live well and are involved in ministry at the tough places of life. People like this are, actually, very rare. Some like to communicate, but their lives are not very reflective of their pulpit concerns. Integrity is the pearl of great price, it would seem.

Ryan Bash can speak. He writes extremely well, he loves family and neighbors and has led his church out to prison ministry. It is the humble estimation of this professor and pastor that we need to hear more from guys like that. This volume is Ryan's response to encouragement to be that man in written form. He has responded well.

He writes this book as a young man, fresh from receiving his Master's degree from seminary. The Lord has therefore taught him much, and will teach him much more. I can't wait to see, over the next several decades, what the Lord will do through Ryan's ministry, his family and his churches. It will be exciting.

But it needn't be large.

Ryan writes from the vantage point that has convinced him that "exciting" is being who God wants you to be and accomplishing what Jesus wants you to accomplish. In *Follow Me* the author gives the distinct impression that this needn't be done in a mega-church. It is done with whomever the Lord ranks you with, this country or that one, a larger church or a smaller one, a new ministry or the extension of a legacy.

But it must be done. Abandonment to Jesus' challenge of "Follow Me" is the stuff of greatness, wherever, whenever.

Read on. It will be a treat. But act on the challenges. For then it will be transforming.

Matt Friedeman
Jackson, MS

Introduction

Follow me.

With just two simple words, Jesus altered the course of twelve lives forever. With an extended hand and a gleam in His eye, he invited these men to step out into a life of true adventure: a life fraught with storms, imprisonment, miracles, beatings, feasts, fights, laughter, tears, trials ... and *victory*. He taught them, prayed for them, challenged them, and comforted them; and when His time came to return to the Father, He sent the Holy Spirit to empower them to follow in His steps. His ministry would now become their ministry; his mission, their mission. And so like Him, they would face the scorn of a world in rebellion against God. Like Him, they would pour out their lives for the sake of the lost and broken. Like Him, they were obedient, even unto death.

Jesus fully invested Himself into these men, confident that they could do greater things than even He did (John 14:12), in the power of the Spirit. But before He went willingly to the cross, before He suffered for the redemption of mankind, He lifted His heart toward Heaven and said a prayer for you. He said a prayer for me. He prayed for all of us who would come to believe in Him through the witness and work of these disciples of His. He prayed that we would be one, as Father, Son and Spirit are one; He prayed that we would one day share in His glory, knowing fully the depth of the Father's love. In effect, He was looking past the moment of His prayer – looking into a future which included all of us – and was extending that same invitation to every man, woman and child who would ever live: *follow me.*

It has become commonplace in the church today to talk about being a "follower of Jesus." We sing, pray and testify about the way we love Him. We refer to ourselves as Christians, disciples, and servants; yet, the evidence seems to suggest that such terms are largely devoid of meaning. What I mean is, the *practical behaviors* of professing Christians are often indistinguishable from those of the rest of the world.[1] Ultimately, then, when many of us refer to ourselves as *followers of Christ*, we simply mean that we affirm basic tenets of the Christian faith. Or we mean that we attend church services somewhere. Or maybe even that we *like* Jesus. But are we really following Him? Are we walking with Him, learning from Him, being challenged by Him, and obeying Him, as a disciple would?

I know what you're thinking: here comes another guilt trip! Many of us, if we're impacted by such challenges at all, have trained ourselves to be satisfied with simply *feeling bad* about our low standard of discipleship. We read a book or hear a sermon which challenges us to follow Christ, and we agree. The problem is, seldom do we know what to do about it. We may pray a little harder for a few days, maybe read a little more Scripture (both great ideas, by the way!) for a week. But in the end, we are no more *following* Jesus than were the disciples before they stepped off their boats and out of their prior circumstances. So what can we do?

My hope is that this book serves as a starting point for you to discover the answer. What follows is not a deep, theological treatise on what it means to be a Christian; rather, it is a practical guide for all who wish to truly follow Jesus, but don't quite know where to begin. Whether you are new to the faith, or you simply recognize that, even after years in the church, your stated beliefs have not led to real transformation in your life, I have written this for you. My sole conviction in this project is that we ought to take seriously the words of Jesus, when He said, "if anyone would come after me, he must deny himself and take up his cross daily and follow me" (Luke 9:23, NIV). Do you really believe that, and all that it implies? If so – or even if you're unsure, but at least interested – keep reading.

Before you begin, though, let me say this: some may object that what follows is too much about our *works*. After all, one might argue, we're not saved by the things we do, but by the grace of God! I couldn't agree more. But this book is not about somehow earning a right standing with the Lord; the question before us is simply, *what does it look like to follow Jesus?* Our tendency as evangelicals (yes, this is my theological background, if it helps) is to react sharply

---

[1] George Barna reports, for instance, that we effectively consume the same types of media, give no more of our resources to help the poor, divorce just as frequently, and engage in our communities (volunteering, politics, etc.) to approximately the same extent as non-believers. Barna, G. (1998). *The Second Coming of the Church*. Nashville, TN: Word Publishing, p. 6.

against anything that smacks of a works-based salvation. So much so, unfortunately, that we often prefer to speak of a faith attached to no activity at all. But James called that kind of faith dead (James 2:20). And as my mentor, Dr. Matt Friedeman, is fond of saying, "If we make disciples by sitting around and talking, don't be surprised if our disciples sit around and talk." I don't believe that sort of discipleship is even close to what Jesus imagined when He first said to those twelve men, "*Follow Me.*" So ...

Will reading this book and following all the suggestions make you a Christian? No.

Is this an exhaustive list of all that following Him entails? Of course not.

As you work through this text, will you come to know Christ more intimately, trust Him more completely, and be better-equipped to live a life of real faith, come what may? I certainly hope so.

So read on with a discerning eye. I encourage you to actually put into practice what is suggested at the end of each chapter. And as you do, continually seek the grace of God through prayer and Scriptural study. Wrestle with these ideas in the context of the body of Christ, not just as an individual. And above all things, remember that He did not just invite us to *follow*. He said, follow *ME*. The call was not simply to a robotic adherence to a set of rules; He called them (as He does us) *to Himself.* As you are ever mindful of that, I pray that He uses these practical steps to help usher you into the life of adventure He's envisioned for you.

Oh, and don't neglect the footnotes – many of them help tell the story.

Ryan Bash

Contents

Letting Go

I drew a quick breath as I worked my way beyond the railing of the bridge, looked down at the water so many feet below, and wondered if I could really go through with it. I was terrified of heights to be sure, but I was absolutely determined to jump. My heart was already racing as I walked from the car to the bridge; but it wasn't until I maneuvered my body through its protective structure that I really began to doubt. Suddenly, as there was now nothing between me and this terrifying plummet, my knuckles turned white. My breaths were short, my pulse had quickened, and my arms were slightly shaking. One step, and I'd be on my way down. One step, and there would be no turning back. One step, and *everything* would change. Could I really let go? How did I even get to this point?

Ninety minutes earlier, I was in my dorm room spending the afternoon as I usually did – with my nose in the books. While the rest of my friends were throwing a Frisbee in the middle of campus, talking to girls on the green, or dominating the latest version of Madden NFL on Sega Genesis, I was frantically scanning my syllabi, nervous I had neglected to read a page of the assigned text. Yep, I was *that* guy.[1] So as was my custom on a weekday afternoon, I was diligently doing my homework, so that later on in the evening I could … go to bed early. Don't judge me.

With my highlighter in hand and my book before me, my heart nearly stopped when my door burst open. It was my friend Carlton. Looking like he'd sprinted to my room, and with his eyes

---

[1] Ok … I still am that guy. I can't help it.

ablaze, he spoke seven words that changed my life: "We're jumping off a bridge! You in?"

"Um ... no? I choose life."

"Come on, a couple guys did it yesterday, and we're going again. Me, you, Russ, Shannon, and Frank (Franco). It'll be awesome!"

Immediately, twelve reasons came into my mind as to why I needed to pass. Good reasons. Unfortunately, this is the only one that came out: "I've got homework." Oops. I'm sure I had better reasons than that. Carlton quickly rolled his eyes. And for the next five minutes, he either made a convincing case, guilt-tripped me, or secretly drugged me. I don't really remember the circumstances that led to me saying yes. I only remember speeding around Nicholasville, Kentucky in Shannon's little white car, with Rage Against the Machine blaring on the speakers.[2] As testosterone filled the car like smoke, we made a handful of stops before coming to our final destination.

The first bridge was too high. We might actually die from jumping off that one. The second bridge had questionable water levels. But the third bridge ... well, it was just right. So we parked the car and filed out to the ledge. Looking back, I am not quite sure why we deemed this activity safe.[3] But as I recall, at least one of my buddies had been there the day before and knew the water was deep enough. Somehow, as scared as I was at the thought of stepping off a bridge, the actual preparation to do so was much worse than I'd anticipated. In sharp contrast to the boisterous experience of the drive there, as we worked our way to the ledge, no one was saying anything.

Our silence was broken by the lone concerned citizen on the bank of the river. Some poor woman was just sitting there on a lawn chair doing some fishing that afternoon, when five shirtless buffoons stepped out onto the edge of the bridge above her. She didn't ask us what we were doing, who we were, or anything like that. She just gave us a half-hearted, "Don't do it, guys."[4] Most of us didn't really

---

[2] Admittedly, not exactly choice listening for five young Christian guys, but we were trying to get pumped up, I guess.

[3] Is this a good time to mention to the reader that this was an absolutely horrible idea? Kids, don't do this.

[4] For what it's worth, this has always been my favorite memory of that day. Did she feel like she had to say that? Was she genuinely concerned for us?

know how to respond. Briefly, I considered screaming, "Thank you, Mommy!" and running into the safety of her anonymous arms (did I mention I was terrified?). But just in time to save me the humiliation, Franco (with eyes still on the water) answered back, "We're good, thank you." That seemed to satisfy our bystander.

So there we were, all five of us standing on the ledge, uncertain as to how to proceed. Finally, one of us asked, "Who's going first?"

With his eyes fixated on the water below, Shannon solemnly responded, "I got this." And with that, he let go and stepped off, as the rest of us held our breath.

———————

*As Jesus was walking beside the Sea of Galilee, he saw two brothers, Simon called Peter and his brother Andrew. They were casting a net into the lake, for they were fishermen. "Come, **follow me**," Jesus said, "and I will make you fishers of men." At once they left their nets and followed him. Going on from there, he saw two other brothers, James son of Zebedee and his brother John. They were in a boat with their father Zebedee, preparing their nets. Jesus called them, and immediately they left the boat and their father and followed him. (Matthew 4:18-22)* [5]*

What do you imagine the scene was like that day along the Sea of Galilee, when Jesus passed by and invited Simon, Andrew, James and John to follow Him? For most of my life, this passage barely registered as a blip on my radar. Sure, it was momentous in that it served as the official calling of the Lord's inner circle. It is a meaningful moment because it was the launching point of their journey together, but the scene itself (at least in my mind), was relatively bland. Jesus walks by and invites these men to follow after him; He makes a strange comment about how they'll be *fishing for people*, and the men consent. Now they're disciples. Yawn. Now on to the miracles and the cross!

Our tendency, of course, if we approach the text in this fashion, is to subsequently interpret our *own* call to follow Jesus in the same manner. We go to a church service, for example, hear an

————————————————————————

Is she going around somewhere telling this same story from her perspective today? I may never know.

[5] See also Mark 1:16-20 and Luke 5:1-11. All Scriptures are from the NIV, unless otherwise specified.

invitation to accept Christ, and our hearts are warmed. We know we ought to be different, we're tired of being miserable sinners, so we agree. We say the prayer, and now we're safe. Yet, the more I wrestle with this text, the more I am convinced that such an interpretation misses the magnitude of the moment – for them and for us!

Again, as I stated in the Introduction, the question before us is this: *what does it mean to follow Jesus?* For all of us who are anxious to respond to His invitation into genuine discipleship, we must first come to grips with what it means to say yes. Sadly, too many of us are satisfied to relegate this commitment to a basic affirmation of the facts. We assume that saying "yes" means little more than agreeing that God exists, then choosing to be a better person – or at least trying to be. Fortunately, the Scripture saves us from this error. As we delve a little deeper into Matthew 4, what we find is that *their "yes" was a total commitment of everything they had.* It was a full surrender. My hope is that, by the end of this chapter, you and I will be able to determine whether or not the same can be said of us.

Complete Surrender

The place to begin, then, is with what is perhaps the defining characteristic of the "yes" of Simon, Andrew, James and John. More so than anything else we could say of it, their response to the call of Christ was *complete.* First, in the case of Simon and Andrew, the author is careful to note that when Jesus said, "follow me," the two men *left their nets* (v. 20) and went after Him. Again, when the Lord extends the same invitation to James and John, the writer does not merely indicate *that they agreed.* The reader is informed that *they left the boat and their father and followed him* (v. 22).

Pause for a moment and consider the weight of that information. Obviously, all four of these men were fishermen, by trade. These weren't weekend warriors; they weren't retirees enjoying a nice day on the lake – they made a living (perhaps in some cases, supported families) casting nets and bringing in the haul. Simon and Andrew weren't just walking away from a net in verse 20. They were effectively abandoning the only source of security they'd ever known. They were tossing their one means of income into the sea and walking away. Can you imagine?

For James and John, the complete abandonment of this moment was not just *financially* irresponsible, but it was also incredibly personal. They weren't just preparing nets with their boss and some colleagues. This was the family business. They were there with their father, as they likely had been every day, for as long as they could remember. When they jumped ship to follow Jesus, it was quite possibly at the expense of their father's broken heart – or even his rage. The point is that when they stepped off their boats, they weren't just risking a belly-flop injury on the way down. They were sacrificing their financial security, their familial relationships, and their futures, just to name a few. What lay ahead for them in the company of this Jesus was likely a bit of a mystery, and there was no guarantee that all of this would be waiting for them, if and when it all went south.

My friend Stu often shares the story of what others might dub "the stupidest decision of his life." He was serving as the youth pastor at a Methodist church, and by all accounts[6] he was beloved there. The ministry was thriving, he had good relationships with the pastor, the students, and the families, and life was great. Then one day, a still, small voice came to him saying, "Stu, it's time to go." So sudden and surprising was this message, that it took him off guard. Go where, he wondered? Time to go to lunch? "No, Stu, it's time to go."

Very quickly, Stu recognized that it was the Lord, and that "time to go" meant that it was time to step away from his position at the church. There was just one problem: he didn't exactly have another job offer. What he did have was a wife and two children to support. Now, most of us would have cut the voice off right then, but Stu was certain it was the Lord. But was the Lord crazy?! Stu decided to seek the counsel of a trusted advisor, whose sage advice was as follows: "Don't be an idiot. You've got a family to support, and if you walk away, you have nothing. You're probably hearing wrong, don't do it."

Nevertheless, Stu was certain about what the Lord was speaking. So Stu resigned his position. The first time I heard this story, I was certain that the next part would go something like this: "So the VERY next day, I got a call from a megachurch, and they wanted to pay me a kajillion dollars to oversee their teen ministry with 2,000 students. Glory be to God." But that's not what came next. What came next was *nothing*. No job offer, no job opportunities, no way to support his family through ministry. So, Stu took care of his family doing whatever he could. He soon landed at

---

[6] Ok, just his account, but still.

the seminary where he'd recently received a Master's degree, accepting a position to sweep their gym floors. Even some of the students there who knew him couldn't help but express their surprise that *this* was the job his degree had landed him.

In all of this, Stu couldn't quite see what the Lord was doing. But that didn't stop him from surrendering all. Before long, Stu took a position with a local Christian college, which eventually led to him being the head of Campus Ministries there. And in that role, he went on to directly impact the lives of thousands of young men and women preparing for ministry all over the world. That's how I met Stu. And I would not be overstating the facts to suggest that his example of faithfulness and courage has transformed my understanding of discipleship. I often wonder what my life would be like today had not one man made the "foolish" decision to walk away from a well-paying job, with no foreseeable means to support his family.

C. S. Lewis has noted that our ordinary idea of Christianity looks something like this: We first adopt as our starting point our current selves. Then, we admit that something else – something moral – has a claim on this self. We must therefore start "being good" and give up certain behaviors which we call "wrong." However, he continues:

> we are hoping all the time that when all the demands have been met, the poor natural self will still have some chance, and some time, to get on with its own life and do what it likes ... [but] Christ says, 'Give me All. I don't want so much of your time and so much of your money and so much of your work: I want You ... Hand over the whole natural self, all the desires which you think innocent as well as the ones you think wicked – the whole outfit.'[7]

Simon, Andrew, James and John left everything. They walked away from job security, from family, from future plans, from years of training, and from all they'd ever known. In that moment, Jesus had all of them.

---

[7] Lewis, C. S. (Revised 2001). *Mere Christianity*. San Francisco, CA: HarperCollins.

Immediate Surrender

Not only did these four men offer themselves *completely*, but they did so *immediately*. Again, it's in verses 20 and 22 where we see this. Simon and Andrew left their nets *at once*. James and John left the boat *immediately*. One of my favorite scenes in the movie *Forrest Gump* takes place on the water. Forrest has finally achieved the dream of his dearly departed friend Bubba by acquiring his own "shrimpin' boat." He is living a quiet life, hauling in shrimp, when he gets an unexpected visitor. It's his acerbic leader from his days in the army, Lieutenant Dan. Forrest is moving along in the boat, when he looks out onto the dock and sees Lieutenant Dan sitting there smiling from his wheelchair. Forrest, delighted to see his old friend, and without any other preparation, just takes an awkward leap into the water, as his now-unmanned boat goes crashing into the pier. An immediate response, to say the least.

I love this scene, because it's how I picture the reaction of these four disciples. When Jesus called, there was no hesitation. We almost get the impression that Simon and Andrew may have literally cast a net into the Sea of Galilee, then jumped in after it, leaving others to tend to it. Luke's account of these events suggests that they at least had the good sense to bring the boats ashore (5:11). Either way, neither the net nor the fish were any longer their concern. But what about James and John? The text reveals that they were not alone in their vessel. They left both their father and hired men (Mark 1:20) with the boat to join Jesus.

For years, this one piece bothered me. I mean, this life of adventure with Christ was great for James and John, but in the process, they left their father with little more than a "So long, pops!" Dallas Willard says, "Imagine doing that today. How would family members, employers, and coworkers react to such abandonment? Probably they would conclude that we did not much care for them … Did not Zebedee think this as he watched his two sons desert the family business to keep company with Jesus?"[8] Without a doubt, it does seem careless. It does seem too abrupt. It does seem a bit … impulsive.

In my days as a youth pastor, I had the opportunity to meet a number of interesting people. One such person was a man from the community named Maris. Normally, given my particular position, he and I would likely have not crossed paths. But he stopped by our

---

[8] Willard, D. (1991). *The Spirit of the Disciplines: Understanding How God Changes Lives.* San Francisco, CA: HarperCollins, p. 261.

church on a Friday, which happened to be the one day everyone else on staff had off, except for me. Unfortunately for Maris, who came expressing an urgent need, I was the only one available. Maris was incredibly friendly but indicated that he was in deep despair. It was almost Christmas, he had several children at home, and he didn't have anything to give them for gifts.

Our church policy at the time was to take benevolence needs through the office and through a committee, if necessary. So while Maris waited, I went to the office to see what we could do. Sadly, our options there were limited to gift cards for the local gas station – not exactly what he needed. I wasn't sure what to do, so I started collecting things from my office that he could give to his children – an event t-shirt, a free tote I'd received, a book, some toys.[9] I gave him everything I could think would be useful. I wanted to help, but it was a truly pathetic effort. So eventually, Maris kindly asked me if I could take him to the store to pick up a few toys. At this point, I was getting a little irritated ("come on guy, I gave you a XXL t-shirt for your toddler, what more do you want?"), and I said, "Maris, that's all the church can do."

But Maris looked at me and said, "I'm not asking what the church can do. I'm asking for your help. *You*, pastor Ryan."

"I don't know what else I can do, Maris."

And then he said it: "How about those hundreds in your pocket?"

Pause. I almost never carry cash with me. It's incredibly rare. In fact, it's a good day if I have a dollar in my pocket. But on this particular day, I had earlier cashed a check for $500. My wife and I had earmarked it for something, but the point is that I happened to have hundreds in my pocket at that time. Five of them. Maris had no way of knowing this, as they were buried deep. So when he said it, my face froze up like a statue. My mouth was open and everything. A thousand thoughts were racing through my head. How did he know? Can Maris read minds? Can I outrun Maris if I have to? Should I start running now? Wait – is this you, Lord? What should I do? Do you want me to change my plans with this money, Lord?

Unfortunately, Maris left me an out. As he mentioned the hundreds, he let out a little laugh as though he might be joking. When I found my voice again, I pretended that he was. So I let out

---

[9] What can I say? Youth pastors collect strange things during the course of ministry.

8

the mother of all awkward, nervous laughs. And with only a few seconds to reconsider that crazy notion of giving up MY money, I restated my regret that there was nothing else I could do. Maris kindly said, "Ok," thanked me for the crummy, used things I gave him (my assessment, not his), and went on his way. I've never seen him again.

Now you may be thinking to yourself, "What a relief! Only an idiot would give cash to a man off the street!" Maybe so. But if I am certain of nothing else about that day, it's that God was prompting me to help in some way. God had equipped me to help with cash I wasn't expecting. And instead of diving in with an immediate "yes," I slowed down, talked myself out of it, and kept money that didn't truly belong to me. By the end of the day, I came to so hate that cash that I would have given it to the first person who asked. Again, the issue is not how a church or an individual ought to navigate benevolence resources. The question is whether or not we're going to be faithful to the Lord's call *right now*, or if we'll hesitate just long enough to talk ourselves out of it.

I imagine that if James and John had paused to ask their father, he may have given them lots to think about. He could have helped them weigh the pro's and con's, if he was so inclined. He may have even forbidden them to leave. We can only guess, because what they did instead was to leave immediately. They didn't question the call, they didn't stop and consider what was best for everyone involved. They just stepped off and went with Jesus; because, as Willard concludes, being with Him "was the only possible doorway to discipleship."[10]

Surrender to Receive

As Luke reports in his account of these events (5:11), the disciples left *everything* to follow Jesus. And they did so immediately, without hesitation. But all of this begs the question, *why*? Why would these men abandon all to follow Him? Most scholars agree that this was not the first time these men had encountered Jesus. For instance, John 1:35-42 is widely regarded as an initial invitation to Simon and Andrew, prior to the scene at the lake.[11] But still – to leave *everything*? To go without second thought or hesitation? Why?

---

[10] Willard, p. 261.
[11] Carter, C. [Gen. Ed.]. (1966). *The Wesleyan Bible Commentary, Vol. IV*. Grand Rapids, MI: Baker Books, p. 29.

The key to understanding, in my estimation, is the invitation itself. Look again at what Jesus said: "Come, follow me, and I will make you *fishers of men.*" Our tendency is to presume that the only thing Jesus calls us to abandon is *sin* (in the active, behavioral sense). And surely he does. So when we consider this call to the disciples, we are quick to equate it with an invitation to the utterly lost. But the thrust of this text speaks to a different issue. For you see, Jesus never condemns fishing, as a trade, here. It's not so much the life of sin (as we commonly speak of it) from which He is calling them out – as there is nothing inherently wrong with being a fisherman.

What He is effectively telling them is that *if you leave all of this to follow me, I will take what you are and redeem it for my glory. If you hand over control of everything – even the desires, plans and pursuits which you deem to be innocent* (so says Lewis) – *I will give you something even better. I will give you a part of my redemptive ministry in this world, and you will be casting nets for the eternal rescue of humanity.* Ultimately, then, the call to follow Jesus is not simply an invitation for the lost to say the sinner's prayer and be done with it. It runs much deeper than that. It's an extended hand to those of us who may know *about* Him, but who are nevertheless continuing to follow our own pursuits. It's a call to those of us who are still operating on our own terms, to come and find a higher purpose – His purpose. But to follow Him requires all. To be His disciple demands that we give up everything ... "yes, even [our] own lives" (Luke 14:26, 33).

So what about you? Have you surrendered all to follow Him? Consider first your relationships: does Christ have your allegiance above all other people? Are you fully obedient to what the Scripture teaches about marriage, purity, and submission to your spouse? Or have you compromised your integrity to keep another person happy? Does pride prevent you from serving those around you – be it a spouse, a co-worker, a neighbor or (gulp) an enemy? Or will you, like Christ, empty yourself for the sake of others? Or how about you, parents? Does the word of Christ dwell richly in your household? Are your children learning to serve the Lord, not just from their Sunday school teachers, but from you? Or do sports and extra-curricular activities steer the ship of your family schedule? Are you more concerned with their comfort and happiness, or with their relationship with Jesus? Is He the Lord of all your relationships?

What about your attitudes? Does He have all of those? Have you turned your back on your prejudices, your anger, and your demand for control? Do you love Him so deeply that you love the people He loves? Do you see others through His eyes, or only as the world sees them? Do you love the poor, the diseased and broken? I'm not asking whether or not you tear up at the sight of a heart-wrenching infomercial on world hunger. Do you actually reach out and help? Do you extend your hand to them? Or how about your political preferences? Do your positions on the economy, on gun control, on foreign affairs, immigration, and the sanctity of life and marriage come directly from His teaching? Or have you formed your opinions without His input? He says, "I want ALL of you."

Take a look at your dreams and desires. Is He the Lord of your career? Or do you simply follow the money? Do the passions and concerns of Christ determine how you plan for retirement? How you decide what to purchase? How do you advise your children to plan for their futures? Does your greatest aspiration in life have anything to do with the Kingdom of God? Or are you hoping that He can simply see fit to use you in the path you're already determined to follow? Jesus didn't ask these men if He could come and join them. He said, "follow me." Follow me, and I'll do something far greater with your life than you could ever imagine.

What about your habits? Is Christ the Lord of your free time? *Wait – you mean I can't play ball anymore? I can't go fishing? I can only read the Bible and pray?!* Calm down. Allow me to explain: some habits have no place in the life of a follower of Christ. Some of the things that we put before our eyes and ears with regularity are grieving the Holy Spirit in the truest sense. Some of us are doing damage to our minds and bodies and we need to repent. But even our harmless habits have the capacity to distract us from the mission for which He placed us on this earth. As near as I can tell, Jesus loved to celebrate. He delighted in His friends and in laughter – so much so that He was often accused of being a party animal.[12] But in all of His activities, His eye was firmly centered on the rescue of humanity and the glory of the Father. Is yours?

So I ask again: does He have all of you? Have you abandoned your claims to your time, your resources, and your pride? Have you handed over your relationships, your dreams, and your habits? Or are you trying to run after Jesus as you carry all those along with you? Matthew 4 shows us that it doesn't work that way. He either has all of you, or He is not truly Lord. Lay down your nets, stop

---

[12] Does anyone still say "party animal?" No? Just me and the 1980's?

trying to please others, and step off the boat. It doesn't happen when we try to cling to who we were – even the seemingly harmless parts – then add on Christ. So says Lewis:

> *That is exactly what Christ warned us you could not do ... If I want to produce wheat, the change must go deeper than the surface. I must be ploughed up and resown ... And the first job each morning consists simply in ... letting that other, larger, stronger, quieter life come flowing in ... We can only do it for moments at first. But from those moments the new sort of life will be spreading through our system: because now we are letting Him work at the right part of us. It is the difference between paint, which is merely laid on the surface, and a dye or stain which soaks right through.*

––––––––––––––––

When Shannon stepped off the ledge and hit the water, he vanished from our sight. It felt like he was gone for minutes. But when he finally emerged, as soon as he caught his breath, he let out visceral yell, not unlike a lion's roar. He had let go of the bridge, stepped into the unknown, and he had emerged victorious. It was apparently enough to empower the rest of my friends. Because without a word, Russ jumped next, then Carlton after him. Both men reacted in the same way. Franco took his turn next, until I was left standing alone on the bridge. After watching my four friends, I was slightly more confident that I might not die, but no less afraid of the drop. If I let go of this bridge, there was no turning back. If I took one step forward, whatever happened next was out of my control. As my friends were soaked and beaming at me in the water below, I knew I could wait no longer. It was time to let go.

So in one motion, before I could talk myself out of it, my hands released the bridge, I stepped forward with my right foot, and then I plummeted for an hour and a half. Or at least it felt like it. When I finally hit the water and realized I wasn't dead, I couldn't wait to emerge at the surface. Because now I had my own roar to release.

Victory.

Of course jumping off a bridge is a horrible idea. Any child knows that. But when I came out of that water, I was a new man. I realized I no longer had to be controlled by fear. I realized that with

12

great risk comes great reward. Eventually I came to more fully understand that God has invited me on a grand adventure with Him, and that every day it will require that I take a step of faith, trusting that He'll do something amazing, even if I can't see it.

And to think, all I had to do was let go.

Practical Action Step

Nothing says "first step" like *total* surrender, right? Don't be overwhelmed. The call is complete, but even complete surrender starts somewhere. Perhaps, as you read this chapter, some area of your life came to mind. Maybe you've already become aware of a particular relationship, attitude, desire or habit which you've kept from the Lordship of Christ. If not, stop reading and pray now; ask Him to show you the greatest stronghold in your heart – that one arena of your life which you've refused to surrender to Him. Just be careful: if you ask in all sincerity, He will surely give you an answer. When He does, say "yes" immediately. Whatever He is telling you to abandon or embrace so that you can follow Him, do it. Don't just *commit* to saying yes, don't just *plan* to do it. Go do it now.

Canceling Debts

On Monday morning, October 2, 2006, a gunman entered a one-room Amish school in Nickel Mines, PA. In front of 25 horrified pupils, thirty-two-year-old Charles Roberts ordered the boys and the teacher to leave. After tying the legs of the ten remaining girls, Roberts prepared to shoot them execution-style with an automatic rifle and four hundred rounds of ammunition that he brought for the task. The oldest hostage, a thirteen-year-old, begged Roberts to "shoot me first and let the little ones go." Refusing her offer, he opened fire on all of them, killing five and leaving the others critically wounded. He then shot himself as police stormed the building. His motivation? "I'm angry at God for taking my little daughter," he told the children before the massacre.

The story captured the attention of broadcast and print media in the United States and around the world. By Tuesday morning some fifty television crews had clogged the small village of Nickel Mines, staying for five days until the killer and the killed were buried ... The blood was barely dry on the schoolhouse floor when Amish parents brought words of forgiveness to the family of the one who had slain their children. The outside world was incredulous that such forgiveness could be offered so quickly for such a heinous crime...

Fresh from the funerals where they had buried their own children, grieving Amish families accounted for half of the seventy-five people who attended the killer's burial. Roberts' widow was deeply moved by their presence as Amish families greeted her and her three children. The forgiveness went

14

beyond talk and graveside presence: the Amish also supported a fund for the shooter's family.[1]

As these victimized Amish families humbly modeled genuine forgiveness, the world looked on in awe. Even many Christians, who ought to understand something about grace and forgiveness, struggled to comprehend how these parents could offer such love after losing what was most precious to them. Hence, this model, playing out before our eyes, caused many to look inside themselves and ask those difficult questions: if it were me, if this was my little girl ... could I forgive? Could I attend the funeral of the man who'd slain my child, extend genuine condolences to his family, and then make sacrifices to support them in their grief?

Just over six years later, I was working at a fire station in rural Ohio, shortly before Christmas. It was a Friday morning, and I was finishing a task when my co-worker turned on the news. Though I was only half-listening at first, the images in front of me quickly grabbed my attention. From a helicopter above, the cameras were showing scenes of an elementary school, as armed officers of the law moved quickly in and around the building. The location, I would come to learn, was Sandy Hook Elementary, in Newtown Connecticut. Though details were at first a bit uncertain, the picture became clearer as the day unfolded: Twenty children (mostly ages 6 and 7) and six adults had been shot dead. The shooter had subsequently taken his own life. And just as these details were emerging, before I could fully wrap my mind around what had just taken place, I had to leave the fire station to take my own six-year-old daughter to school. For some time after that day, as I wept for these families, I found myself looking inside once again and asking that question: if it were my little girl, could I ever forgive?

———————

We have just begun to explore what it looks like to follow Jesus. And as terrifying as it can be to jump from the security of our "boats" into the unknown with Christ, there is most certainly a sense of adventure about it. Don't get me wrong: it's not easy to completely surrender all that we are and all that we desire for the

---

[1] Kraybill, D., Nolt, S. & and Weaver-Zercher, D. (2007). *Amish Grace: How Forgiveness Transcended Tragedy.* Hoboken, NJ: Jossey-Bass, *excerpts from back cover.*

sake of Christ ... but if we believe that He can truly do something even greater with our lives, we can experience a real confidence, even in submission. Jumping from that bridge was terrifying, yes, but exhilarating all at the same time.

But once our feet hit the water, so to speak, what we find is that this life into which we've now entered includes more than just *me and Jesus*. What we find is that, though we were expecting to land in the crystal-clear water of "walking with the Lord," what we experience instead is a big messy *splat*! For to follow Jesus is to follow Him into the depths of a sinful world.

It is telling, isn't it, that when the Pharisee asked Jesus about the most important command in the Law (Matt. 22:34-40), the Teacher gave him more than he expected? Upon hearing this question (designed, of course to test him), Jesus answered: "'Love the Lord your God with all your heart and with all your soul and with all your mind.' This is the first and greatest commandment." Hmm, the man must have thought, that's actually pretty good. And perhaps turning back to his cohorts to scheme again, Jesus stops him short. "Oh, and there is another one, would you like to hear it?" The man turns again, begrudgingly obliging. "Sure," he may have muttered. "By all means."

"And the second one is like it," He said, smiling kindly. "'Love your neighbor as yourself.' All the Law and the Prophets hang on these two commandments." And with that, Jesus drove home a very profound truth – one which far too many of us are more than ready to neglect today. And the truth is this: to love Jesus is to love my fellow man. Put another way, I cannot speak of my own reconciliation with God, if I refuse to be reconciled to my neighbor. The two go hand-in-hand. All the Law and all the Prophets hang, not on just one of these commands, but on both together. They're a package deal.

Sadly, for some of us, that comes as particularly bad news, because *other people* can be pretty horrible. They disappoint us. They fail us. They betray us. And in some cases, they damage us deeply – irreparably, it seems. But *knowing that*, Jesus still said this: "If you do not forgive men their sins, your Father will not forgive your sins" (Matt. 6:15). For any one of us who has ever been hurt by another person, this statement ought to give us pause. We sing and rejoice about a merciful God who readily forgives our iniquities, and rightly so. But our Lord made clear that our own forgiveness cannot be secured while we choose to withhold mercy from our fellow man.

In light of that, I would submit to you that *to follow Jesus demands that we forgive.* To be honest, for some, this may prove to be the most difficult challenge presented to you in this book. Learning to forgive others is no small hurdle; but, I would suggest to you that, until we submit to Christ in this area of our lives, the rest of our efforts are rather fruitless. Jesus went so far as to say[2] that even if you are at the altar, offering your gift to the Lord, and you recall that there is conflict between you and your brother, leave it! Go reconcile, go fix it! In other words, your offering is worthless if you are not reconciled to one another. It's *that* important! So, then, we ask, what does it mean to truly forgive?

———————————

Peter had likely been walking with the Lord long enough now where he must have imagined that he had a pretty good handle on what would impress Him. Jesus had been teaching on what to do if a brother sins against you, while Peter just nodded knowingly. So at the first opportunity, Peter stepped forward and patted himself on the back, in the form of a question. "Lord," he asked, how many times should I forgive my brother when he sins against me? Up to seven, do you think?"

Peter couldn't even pretend to wipe the grin off his face. I mean, *seven*! Who else is offering seven?! In rabbinic circles, the general consensus was that a brother ought to be forgiven for a repeated sin three times; by the fourth, the well was tapped – no more forgiveness was required.[3] Peter was blowing that number out of the water! He braced himself for the spirited affirmation from Jesus, which was sure to come. Stand back, boys, this may be slightly embarrassing for all of us.

And then it sort of was. Only not in the way Peter had envisioned. "No, Peter, not seven times, but rather, seventy-seven times."[4] What?! And like all of us, Peter was reminded once again

———————————

[2] Matthew 5:23-26.
[3] Carson, D. (1984). *The Expositor's Bible Commentary, Vol. 8* [Gaebelein, F., Gen. Ed.]. Grand Rapids, MI: Zondervan, p. 405.
[4] Some prefer here, "seventy times seven." In the end, it doesn't much matter which the reader chooses, as the mathematical figure is hardly the point. Interestingly, we've seen this connection between 7 and 77 before, in Genesis 4:24: "If Cain is avenged seven times, then Lamech seventy-seven times." Carson (p. 405) notes that what Jesus has done is to take an OT

that God's mercy runs so much deeper than our best attempts. To explain, Jesus proceeded to carefully craft a parable of forgiveness. And as He did, He made clear that true healing requires that we gain proper perspectives of ourselves, of God's unsurpassed mercy, and of what it really means to forgive one another.

Know Yourself

> *Therefore, the kingdom of heaven is like a king who wanted to settle accounts with his servants. As he began the settlement, a man who owed him ten thousand talents was brought to him. Since he was not able to pay, the master ordered that he and his wife and his children and all that he had be sold to repay the debt. The servant fell on his knees before him. "Be patient with me," he begged, "and I will pay back everything"* (Matthew 18:23-26).

Perhaps the first idea which Jesus sought to establish with Peter (and all who were listening, both then and now) was a clear picture of his own spiritual reality. Unfortunately, far too few of us have a good grasp of who we really are. As I discovered just recently, my nine-year-old son does not have that problem. While he was off in an adjoining room, reading a book, his younger sister was tattling on her friend to my wife. She was going on and on, expressing (read: *faking*) frustration that her friend had the audacity to call her big brother "annoying." She didn't just pass this information on to my wife, but she did so loudly, making sure her brother could overhear. Immediately, I was concerned, as my son can be a bit sensitive. The girl in question was a mutual friend, and I didn't want his feelings to be needlessly hurt over another child's comment. So quickly, I hushed my daughter, indicating that she didn't need to talk about it, all the while hoping that my son would be protected from hearing this conversation, the content of which was sure to crush him. Much to my surprise, without entering the room or even expressing the slightest bit of dismay, my son chimed in from his chair: "No, it's ok, Dad. I can be very annoying at times." Okay then.

It's hard not to appreciate a self-aware young man. Sadly, this is a trait very few of us ever acquire – particularly when it comes

---

principle of vengeance and transformed it into a principle of forgiveness. His correction of Peter's offering, then, serves not to provide a new number, but to expand his vision of forgiveness.

to our own sinfulness. Sure, if we were engaged in some "really bad things" before we met Christ, we're glad to recognize them for what they were. We'll happily thank God for rescuing us from the *miry clay*; maybe we'll even go so far as to suggest that we didn't deserve His forgiveness. But beyond that ... I mean, is it really *that* bad that I passed along that unflattering story I heard about my co-worker? Is it the end of the world that I spent a few minutes fantasizing about that beautiful woman? Sure, I was a little disrespectful to my parents, or I acted selfishly with my spouse; but, it's not like I murdered anyone! It's not like sold drugs to minors or was violent towards baby kittens!

We all have our own lists of what's really bad, and what's no big deal. But more often than not, we find ourselves excusing (or belittling) our sin against God, either because it doesn't seem quite as bad as the sin of our neighbors, or because ... well, He's God, and forgiveness is His business! So we offer up a half-hearted apology, expecting that God will let it slide (because He *has* to, right?), as we return to whatever we were doing before.

But then Jesus invades that thought process and says, wait a minute. You need to understand just who you are. That's precisely what these first few verses are about for the reader.[5] The first element we must note in this section is the *amount of the debt*. When it came time for the king to settle accounts, a man came before him who owed him *ten thousand talents*. Hold on for a second. How much? Some translations of the Scripture attempt to help you out by suggesting a modern-day equivalent. Unfortunately, between inflation and value changes over time, such numbers can quickly become obsolete. So how do we get a handle on the amount of debt this servant had incurred?

D. A. Carson suggests that we would be wise to think of it in terms of earning power. A common value assigned to a talent, he points out, is six thousand denarii.[6] A denarius, then, is what a common laborer could expect to earn in one day (see Matt. 20:2, for instance). Thus, a talent, Carson concludes, is what an average joe, a

---

[5] Not so sure that the first servant is you? Notice what Jesus says at the end of the story, in verse 35: "This is how my heavenly Father will treat each of you unless you forgive your brother from your heart." Fortunately, He was kind enough to clarify the role assignments at the end of the parable: the king is the Heavenly Father, the wicked servant is you, the second servant is your brother. It's hard to wriggle out of that one.
[6] Carson, p. 516.

blue collar worker, could expect to earn over the course of 20 years. Now think about this for a moment. This servant stood before the king, owing not just 20 years worth of wages (1 talent), but 200,000 years (10,000 talents[7])! But if you absolutely need a figure before we move on, even a modest estimate of what a day-laborer could expect to make today would put the total around 3 billion dollars.[8] But again, that's for a man in his line of work. A more accurate way to place a relevant number on it for you would be to multiply your own yearly salary by 200,000.

As you recover from those figures, now consider the second implication of this section of Jesus' story: the *helplessness* of the servant in light of his debt. Question: what are your options with a multi-billion dollar debt hanging over your head? Answer: you have none. The master's solution, of course, was to order that he and his wife and his children (plus all that they owned) be sold into slavery to repay the debt.[9] But the servant grabbed at one final straw: pity. He fell on his knees in an act of humility and submission. He simply begged. "Be patient," he cried, "and I'll pay back everything." He had no other recourse but to recognize his own helplessness and seek the mercy of the king.

The man owed *infinity*, for all intents and purposes; and therefore, he was utterly helpless. So ask yourself this: how does a man even incur a debt equivalent to 200,000 years' worth of wages? I'm not sure I could do that if I tried. And yet, I am reminded here that I *have* done it, in a spiritual sense. So have you. We all have. It doesn't matter whether you've murdered, passed gossip, or something in between. The moment you and I turned our faces from God and rejected the promptings of the Holy Spirit, we sinned against a perfect, holy God. In so doing, we rendered ourselves incapable of entering His presence, because in Him is no sin.

So in that sense, it matters not how we would subjectively rate the weight of our sin; what matters is that we now owe a debt to

---

[7] For what it's worth, the word used in the Greek text to describe the talents is μυρίων. While 10,000 is the number assigned to it, it can also mean "innumerable" or "countless."

[8] Just think! In only 7,000 years of working, you too can be a billionaire! As long as you have no bills and pay no taxes.

[9] This, of course, does not *actually* repay the debt. In that culture, no servant was worth even close to that amount in the marketplace. Effectively, the only recourse for the master was to literally require everything.

our Maker which is beyond our capacity to repay. Our sins have separated us from God, and our only recourse is to humbly fall at His feet and beg for mercy. Not just for the drug-pedaling, kitten-murdering fiend; but also for the pride-filled church-goer who mostly avoids bad behavior. We are all in debt, and we all need his mercy. Until we truly accept the weight of our sin against God, we do not really know ourselves. Nor can we begin to truly comprehend forgiveness.

Know Mercy

So first, we must know ourselves, and the picture isn't pretty. The good news, however, is that God does not leave us there. Neither does Jesus' story:

> *The servant's master took pity on him, canceled the debt and let him go (v. 27).*

It's just one verse, but we cannot miss the weight of it. Not only is it the best possible news we could hope to receive, but it also serves as the model (as we shall soon see) for what forgiveness looks like. So what must we see here? First, note that the master shows *compassion* toward the servant. Upon seeing this broken, helpless man, the king pitied him. Remember – it was the king's money that was spent. However this man managed to rack up a debt of 200,000 years of wages, it was the king himself who was out the money. Nevertheless, when he looked down at this greedy and careless man, this man who was about to lose everything, including his wife and children, the king was not angry. Instead, he was moved to compassion.

It's hard to say why. Part of me wonders if he pitied not only the man's dire circumstances, but also his pathetic attempt to plead for mercy. Did you catch what the servant said? "Please be patient with me, and I will pay back everything!" Really? You're going to pay back 200,000 years' worth of wages? I, for one, would love to see that. But this is what we do, isn't it? Please, Lord, be patient with me. I'll make it up to you. I'll give money to the church. I'll volunteer my time. I'll make sacrifices. Whether we offer those up as a method of repayment, or we simply run a balance sheet in our minds, assuming that all our good deeds more than make up for our sinful attitudes and behaviors, we are effectively communicating to God that we'll make this up to Him.

Undoubtedly, that is more pitiable even than the servant's plea. Regardless of the particular catalyst for the king's pity, we can be certain that his compassion ultimately stemmed from a love for his servant. And because of that love, we encounter the second critical element here: *he canceled the debt.* Notice that He did not say, "Ok, let's get you started on a payment plan." He did not say, "Ok, I'll reduce your debt to something manageable." He simply looked into the eyes of this servant who'd taken billions, and he said: "You are no longer indebted to me. The debt is cancelled. You are a free man!"

Do you know what it's like to be debt-free? Or even to pay off a single loan? It's exhilarating! The thrill of the knowledge that you are financially beholden to no one in this world is difficult to describe, unless you've come out from under heavy debt: it's like walking on a sea of clouds. Imagine, then, the overwhelming joy this man must have experienced in that moment. Just moments ago, his entire family was about to be sold into slavery. Just moments ago, he owed a debt that no average person could possibly repay. And now … he was about to walk out of that room a free man. It's the kind of joyous liberty that could sustain a man for a lifetime. Or so you would think...

Know Better

This is when the story takes a dark turn. In fact, what happens next shocks the conscience. Jesus continues:

> But when that servant went out, he found one of his fellow servants who owed him a hundred denarii. He grabbed him and began to choke him. "Pay back what you owe me!" he demanded. His fellow servant fell to his knees and begged him, "Be patient with me and I will pay you back." But he refused. Instead, he went off and had the man thrown into prison until he could pay the debt (Matt. 18:28-30).

Again, pay attention to the details. Specifically, take note of what is similar and what is different from the first encounter in the parable. First, just like the king in the beginning, this servant now is the one actively seeking out a debtor. He is calling another to account for what is owed him. And when he locates the man, this fellow servant responds in a manner almost identical to the first servant. He falls to his knees, he begs for mercy, and he offers to repay the debt if only patience is granted him. Very subtly, Jesus affirms a reality of human relationships that most of us already know from experience: yes, people do wrong (become indebted) to us; and yes, they too require mercy from us.

In a sense, these two meetings in the parable are parallels. However, what is perhaps of greater significance is their *dis*similarity. First, reflect for a moment on the amounts owed. The servant owed 200,000 years-worth of wages. We can all agree that this is a ludicrous amount. In contrast, his fellow servant owed him 100 denarii. Given Carson's assessment of the monetary value (see above), consider the following: 100 denarii is not *nothing*. My biggest mistake in the times I've preached on this passage was to belittle the amount owed the second servant. The fact is, his counterpart owed him something like 4 months of wages. Calculate that on your own salary, and decide if you would miss it.

My guess is that, of course you would! What was owed him was not *nothing*. In that light, perhaps you need to hear this today: what happened to you, the injury you suffered, it's not meaningless. Someone hurt your feelings, betrayed you, perhaps even abused you. Because of the wrong you suffered, something valuable was stripped of you, and it *matters*. For me or anyone else to suggest otherwise in order to lead you to a place of healing, or to manipulate you into forgiving, is both disgraceful and naïve. There is no need to belittle our pain.

And yet, what Jesus made clear was that there was a vast disparity between what the servant owed and what was owed the servant. This is why it is so critical to embrace the fullness of the first part of the story. Unless we comprehend the greatness of the divide which existed between the Holy One and our sinful selves, we will never properly understand the difference between 10,000 talents and 100 denarii. The latter is not insignificant ... but it cannot approach our debt to the Father.

It is this critical distinction, then, which highlights the inexplicability of the next: in the second encounter, unlike the first, mercy was denied. What shocks the listener is not so much the difference between the amounts owed, as much as the fact that a man who was just forgiven an insurmountable debt would refuse to do the same for his brother. Ironically, when the second man said that he would pay the debt back, he probably could have, at some point! But it wasn't good enough for the greedy servant. So first he choked the man. And when he begged for mercy, the first servant very coldly threw him into prison until the debt could be repaid. Just moments before, he was given the greatest gift a servant could receive; and he celebrated by refusing to pour that grace back out onto others. It's hard to imagine such selfishness and coldness, right? He should have known better ... right?

The Moral of the Story

Once the word got out, Jesus said, the master called his merciless servant back in: *"You wicked servant,"* he said. *"I canceled all that debt of yours because you begged me to. Shouldn't you have had mercy on your fellow servant just as I had on you?"* In anger his master turned him over to the jailers to be tortured, until he should pay back all he owed. (Matt. 18:32-34)

And then Jesus concluded with the application, which at this point likely would have been obvious to the listener: *"This is how my heavenly Father will treat each of you unless you forgive your brother from your heart."* (v. 35)

Let that last statement sink in for a moment. Now consider all those against whom you still carry a debt sheet. Think about the grudges to which you've been clinging, the people you've held at arm's-length, the former friends you just won't let back into your life. Think about the family member you haven't talked to in months (or years), or the ex-husband who betrayed you. Think about all the times you've said something like, "well I'll forgive, but I won't forget." Now read the end of that story again: *"This is how my heavenly Father will treat each of you unless you forgive your brother from your heart."*

Henry Ward Beecher once famously said, "'I can forgive, but I cannot forget,' is only another way of saying, I will not forgive." Forgiveness ought to be like a cancelled note - torn in two, and burned up, so that it never can be shown against one." If you're a child of God, that's what happened to your note of debt: it was torn in two and burned up. Do you recognize the danger of refusing that same mercy to a fellow debtor? Here's another sad irony in this story: the servant sought to punish his debtor by sending him to prison, until the debt could be paid. That may have taken a little while and was probably rather unpleasant. But because of his refusal to show mercy, he was given over to be *tortured*; tortured until he could pay back his own debt. And as we showed earlier, that may as well be just another way of saying "tortured forever."

So I ask you: what is it that you've thus far been unwilling to forgive in another person? What is it that someone has owed you?

What is it that has caused you to imprison them in guilt and/or silence until the debt is paid, or you decide to let them out? We convince ourselves that we've forgiven one another, simply because we're not actively berating them on a daily basis. If we have ceased throwing darts of our own, we tell ourselves, "Oh, I have forgiven," even while we glare, mutter, and refuse to serve. We hold them at a distance, or ignore them completely, and then try to stand before the God who knows our very thoughts before we think them, convincing Him that we've obeyed His call. God knows better. And if you're honest with yourself, you probably know better too.

So what do we do? How do we let go of the pain, the anger, the hatred, and the mistrust? Maybe you've tried before. Maybe you know that there is a grudge buried deep within your heart. You recognize the danger inherent in clinging to it, but no matter what you do, you can't seem to get over it. Here again, we must return to the model that Christ provided for us in the story, as well as in His own life.

Look again at Matthew 18:27: *The servant's master took pity on him, canceled the debt and let him go.* Not long after he spoke these words, Jesus would be looking down on His fellow man from the cross of execution. Luke indicates (23:32-34) that He was being crucified between two criminals. His executioners drove thick nails into His wrists and into His feet. Religious rulers, Roman soldiers, and even one of the criminals mocked Him in His pain. And the midst of all this torture and derision, Jesus saw these broken, sinful creatures and took pity on them. And then He called upon His Father to cancel their debt. "Please, Father, forgive them! They don't know what they are doing!"

In that moment, Jesus – fully God, and fully *man*, mind you – saw them, not as His torturers, but as poor, lost, sinful creatures. As He looked at them, despite the fact that they were literally killing Him (and abusing Him along the way), He was able to see the depth of their need. He understood that their sinfulness wasn't just hurting Him but was damning them as well. He saw them and pitied them. And so, He begged the Father to cancel their debt. *That* is forgiveness: *compassion and cancellation.* "Well," we reason, "that's Jesus! I'm just a regular human. I can't get there." No one said it would be easy. But imagine for a moment that it is indeed possible. What would it look like?

Elisabeth Elliot tells the harrowing story of her experiences with the Auca Indians in the book entitled, *Through the Gates of*

Splendor. Near the end, she relays the details of the tragic murder of her husband Jim, along with four fellow missionaries, as they sought to bring the Gospel to the Auca people. In a surprise attack, these faithful servants were slain by the very people they sought to evangelize. Left behind in the wake of this tragedy were five widows, most of whom also had children as well. She closes the story by sharing some of the prayers and encouragement they received from believers all over the world, ultimately concluding this:

> *Only eternity will measure the number of prayers which ascended for the widows, their children, and the work in which the five men had engaged. The prayers of the widows themselves are for the Aucas. We look forward to the day when these savages will join us in Christian praise. Plans were promptly formulated for continuing the work of the martyrs ... Revenge? The thought never crossed the mind of one of the wives or other missionaries.*[10]

To be honest, I do not know what Elisabeth Elliot's innermost feelings were towards her husband's murderers on the day she lost him. For what it's worth, I do not even know what emotions were swirling around inside Jesus that moment on the cross. What I do know is that both chose to view their debtors through the eyes of the Father. Both were able to look beyond the pain and see the higher purpose of God's redemption in this world. And in light of that, *they canceled the note.* They tore it up. Rather than revenge and hatred, they chose to pray for those who hurt them. And it is in that choice we find forgiveness.

Someone once said that we are never more like Christ than when we are bearing the sins of another. Forgiveness does not necessarily mean that you deny a debt even exists. It doesn't mean that you will not continue to suffer. And it most certainly doesn't have to wait until the pain subsides. It simply means that you choose to walk in the freedom of gratitude. It means that you thank God daily for the infinite debt from which He's liberated you; and because of that, you choose to view all people through His eyes of love, pleading for their forgiveness, as you plead for the strength to forgive them too. *You cannot do this on your own.* It is only through

---

[10] Elliot, E. (1956). *Through the Gates of Splendor.* Wheaton, IL: Tyndale House Publishers, pp. 253-254.

the power of the Holy Spirit that you can see your debtors as God sees them, praying for their healing.

This is not an easy calling, as it requires immense measures of both gratitude and humility. Yet, it is one we must never neglect, "for if you do not forgive men their sins, your Father will not forgive your sins" (Matt. 6:15). As followers of Christ, we forgive much because we have been forgiven more. Or as Thomas Fuller once said, "He that cannot forgive others breaks the bridge over which he must pass himself; for every man has need to be forgiven."

Practical Action Step

This is where the rubber meets the road. We cannot claim that we've forgiven until we've put our commitment into action; and yet, we would be foolish to take on such a challenge without thoroughly covering the situation in prayer. So first, pray that God would break through your heart and enable you to see this person with His eyes. Pray that He would move on your debtor, nurturing a desire in him or her to reconcile. Continue to pray for that person daily; then, let your prayers culminate in action.

For some, this will involve a direct conversation with the person who has injured you (just bear in mind, that this person may also share with you some ways you've hurt him/her too – are you willing to hear that?). For others, such a conversation is not feasible, due to distance or some other circumstance. Perhaps you simply need to write a letter, extending forgiveness (or even seeking it). Finally for others, perhaps your pain was imposed by someone you don't know. Perhaps the injury was of such a nature that direct contact would be ill-advised. This is not going to be the case for most of us, but for some it surely will. So to you I would suggest this: begin praying for your debtor today. Pray that he/she would find Christ. Pray, like Jesus, that the Father would offer forgiveness. Likely, you may not mean it at first, and that's ok; just pray until you do.

Into the Darkness

Throughout my entire childhood, I was thoroughly convinced that there was no more terrifying place to be at night than inside the normally-friendly confines of my church. The sanctuary was a beautiful room, cavernous with its high, vaulted ceiling, as its floor sloped downward towards the front. In the light, it was an impressive sight to behold. But if ever you set foot in there when the lights were off, it was an entirely different story.

From time to time, several of my young friends and I would find ourselves roaming the building during an evening meeting, which our parents were attending together. And like any good stewards of limited resources, those in charge cut off all unnecessary lights when it wasn't a regular service time. I'm sure this was a fiscally responsible practice that continues even today. However, the end result for us children was free reign in a building full of rooms to explore. With this came opportunities to both test your courage and terrify one another under the cloak of darkness.

We would sprint through the halls, playing tag. We would separate into teams for a game of hide-and-go-seek. We would jump out from around dark corners to scare one another. But the moment someone unwittingly fled for safety into the sanctuary, the mood became somber. It was just like a great jungle-chase scene in the movies, when the fleeing character stumbles onto an ancient burial ground, and the natives all slowly (and fearfully) back away: most of us kids knew better than to venture into the sanctuary.

I mean, who knows what could happen inside? Villains or goblins or ... bears? ... could be hiding in any pew. Monsters could be waiting to pounce. Without the lights, it was a complete blackout in there; and the room was so large that you couldn't even count on safety in numbers. We avoided that room at all costs in the dark; but, if ever circumstances dictated that we absolutely had to pass through ... we sprinted for all we were worth. When we got close enough to the door, the faint glow of an exit sign leading to the hallway signaled our freedom. Bursting through any door of that sanctuary was like a deep gulp of air for a drowning man. That room was terrifying.

By the grace of God, many years later, I had the privilege of serving as a youth pastor in that same church. Other than a period of about five years, when I lived in Kentucky and Pittsburgh, that place was like home to me. So many memories would flood in from my childhood, every time I walked through the halls. I remembered playing with the toys in that nursery, I remembered being dazzled by the flannel graphs in those Sunday school classes. I smiled as I stood in the auditorium where we'd played goofy games with our youth group. God had spoken to me at that altar and through many fine ministers. Here I was, a grown man now, surveying this building where I'd spent so much of my childhood, and I remember reflecting on all these places from a new perspective. Yet, despite the updated décor, despite my own maturation process, and despite my new role in leadership, I soon discovered that one reality remained unchanged.

It was a Sunday evening, and somehow I was tasked with shutting down the lights in the sanctuary. It wasn't something I normally did, but I was glad to help ... or so I thought. From the back of the room, one by one, I moved the switches and watched the light grow dim. I was in a bit of a hurry, so without too much thought, I turned off the final light and looked up to make my way down to the exit in the front of the room. But no sooner did I look up than I realized that I couldn't see two feet in front of my face. Immediately I was frozen in my tracks, as my mind raced back to those adventurous days from my childhood. I remembered the chases, the games in the hallways, the pranks we pulled on one another. But more than anything, in that moment, I felt again that wave of familiar terror sweeping over me. A bead of cold sweat trickled down the side of my head. As my mind surged back into the present, only one thought was screaming for my attention: "Run, man!"

And with that, I was off – racing down the middle aisle like my life depended on it. I couldn't see anything, so I knew I had to rely on instinct alone to tell me when I had reached the turn toward the exit. Within seconds, it felt like I had been running for miles, with no end in sight. Finally, sensing that the floor had leveled out, I made a quick dash to the right – bang! I slammed my knee into the front pew. Normally I would have screamed like a baby, but at that moment I didn't care. I'd leave a leg in the front row if I had to, just get me out of there! As I hobbled toward the exit, I finally located that dim red light. I'm almost safe, I thought! Just a few more feet, and I would be in the clear! With all my might, I surged through the door, suddenly realizing that I hadn't taken a breath since I started moving.

I must admit, it was embarrassing enough to burst through the door of the sanctuary, breathing heavily, sweating, and limping like I'd run a marathon, as a couple of confused colleagues looked on. But the real defeat came moments later as I arrived at this depressing reality: *I'm a grown man, and I'm still afraid of the dark.*

As I have reflected on that day over the years, I have often wondered about the source of such fear. Ask a hundred children (or even some adults) about their fear of the dark, and with minor variations in detail, I imagine all the answers are going to be about the same: *we're scared of the dark because we fear something bad is going to happen to us.* It's why we flee the darkness, isn't it? We're afraid that evil is lurking around the corner. We're afraid that danger can spring up without warning. We're afraid of monsters and villains, whether they are real or imagined. And so again, the result is that we run from the darkness. We avoid it at all possible costs.

Perhaps in the context of our physical lives, such a fear is a natural, even protective, instinct. Perhaps many of us have simply been conditioned to fear and avoid darkness. Whatever the reason, at least in that sense, it may not be all bad. However, *I would suggest that this avoidance is highly problematic when the Church adopts the same attitude regarding spiritual darkness.* Like children (and one spineless former youth pastor, see above) in a lightless building, the Church recognizes the inherent danger in the sin-darkened segments of society. We see that evil lurks around every corner, that the monsters of moral depravity can reach out and grab us at any moment. Therefore, we intentionally avoid the dark places of this world. Instead, we are content to gather in the well-lit safety of our homes and sanctuaries, where the darkness can't touch us. And if, by chance, we happen to find ourselves amidst the darkness, we often close our eyes and sprint through, unconcerned about who or what we may bump into – just so long as we can get out of there as quickly as possible.

The inherent flaw with this mindset, of course, is found in our assumption that the "light" places are where we are most likely to find Jesus. But this is clearly not the testimony of Scripture, is it? In fact, when Jesus walked among us, that was the big knock on Him: for a man of God, He sure hangs out with a lot of untouchables, doesn't He? I mean, what kind of self-respecting teacher eats with a tax collector and sinners (Matthew 9)?! Who in their right mind touches a leper (Luke 5)? Even His own disciples were "surprised to see Him talking with a [Samaritan] woman" (John 4:27). And yet there He was. In fact, it seems as though every time people went to look for Jesus, He was moving in and through the dark places of their society, reaching, teaching, touching and caring. Therefore, if you and I are going to accept His invitation to follow, we are going to need to learn to walk into the darkness. As a matter of fact, He said, this is precisely why you were set apart:

> You are the light of the world. A city on a hill cannot be hidden. Neither do people light a lamp and put it under a bowl. Instead they put it on its stand, and it gives light to everyone in the house. In the same way, let your light shine before men, that they may see your good deeds and praise your Father in heaven (Matthew 5:14-16).

Read that again: *you are the light of the world.* Do you really believe that? Do you believe that you have been poured out into the world, in the power of the Holy Spirit, to shine into the darkest places? If that is true, then shouldn't our lives reflect that reality? Let's explore together just what that would look like.

Go Into Dark Places

"*My Night at the Strip Club.*" Of all the titles you might expect to appear on the blog of a minister, this probably wouldn't make the list. So naturally, I was intrigued enough to keep reading. Katie had recently moved away from the Lancaster (Ohio) area, not long after I had done so myself. I had met her while we were both there, each of us serving as the youth pastor of our respective churches. And through the course of a handful of community events, we had a few opportunities to share in ministry together. Katie immediately gained my respect due to her passion for Christ, as well as for the broken and hurting people of our city. In the brief time that I knew her, she was an authentic model of what it meant to follow Jesus. It was a few years later that I came across her blog and noticed this title.

Fearing at first that her move out of Ohio had led to a vastly different lifestyle for my friend, I read on and quickly found my concerns to be unfounded. However, the scene she went on to describe was no less captivating. Having been prompted by the Lord to follow Him into the dark places of her new city, she soon developed a relationship with an exotic dancer at a local strip club.[1] Through the course of time, and prayer with some Christian companions, Katie and her friends were moved to find a way to express the love of Jesus to even more of these dancers. So with much prayer and preparation, they hatched a plan to present gifts to those ladies working at the club. Desiring simply to let them know that they were beautiful and loved by God, they made plans one Friday evening to enter the building and pass out their gift baskets:

> *[My husband,] David and I loaded up the car with 2 huge baskets of gifts and a bundle of roses and headed for Amarillo. I was reciting Psalm 139, and David was playing the theme song to "Mission Impossible." We met up with our friends, said a quick prayer, and drove across the street to the club's already packed parking lot. Walking up to the door we weren't sure we would actually get in, but we were sure that the Lord had it completely.*

> *We entered into a small room with a barred window at one end. I explained to the man that we were there to deliver gifts to the girls, and after checking our ID he let us right in. He pointed us across the bar to the manager who he described as "the huge guy, with the bald tattooed head," ...*

> *With confidence that only comes from God, we crossed the club and walked up to the manager who, of course, pretended not to see me when I tried to talk to him. When he finally (painfully) turned around, he sent us back to the entrance to pay (extra) before we could talk to him. When we were back before him, he told us we couldn't give the girls the gifts. To which I responded that we were going to do it, and that we would like to do it in a way that would honor his wishes. And my jedi-mind-trick must have worked (aka,*

---

[1] Men, please note: this is neither meant to serve as an inspirational nor an instructional sentence for you.

the Lord softened his heart), because he said we could pass out our gifts if we walked around the club and passed them out to the girls on the floor.

Beth and I split up, and spent the next 15 minutes walking around the club passing out the gifts to all the women. They were all very sweet. Most of them wanted to know who we were and why we had come. Many of the men mocked us as we handed the ladies the gifts, some of them made fun of us, and some of them offered us money. We didn't care. We were able to look each woman in the eyes and tell her that we loved her. And that's what we came there to do.

After we had finished handing out the gifts and talking to each of the girls, we talked with one of the dancers who was at the bar. She thanked us for coming and for the gifts, and offered to pass out the rest of the gifts to the girls who had yet to arrive at work. She said something that I can't get out of my head. She said, "No one comes in here. No one cares about us. No one does anything like this for us."[2]

It has been a few years since I first read Katie's story, but I've never been able to forget the words this young woman spoke to her that day: "No one comes in here. No one cares about us. No one does anything like this for us." Why do you suppose that is? Why is she – and millions of others, with her – trudging around in the dark, assuming that no one cares? Perhaps it is because the Church is afraid of being seen in the dark places. Perhaps it is because we don't want to get sullied ourselves. Maybe it is because we have become convinced that if a lost sinner wants to know Jesus, they'll come to church. Or maybe we really just don't care. Whether we say it with our mouths, or simply with our actions, what we communicate with our absence is nothing less than, *"to Hell with you."* And sadly, many of them are getting the message.

You see, for a lot of us, our assumption is that we are never more pleasing to the Lord than when we're faithfully sitting in church. We close our eyes, we pour ourselves into praise, we even nod at the pastor when he looks our way during the sermon; and in all this, we assume that this is the peak of Christianity. We figure that we're never closer to Jesus than when we're in an emotionally

---

[2] Excerpt from http://awhitestoneblog.wordpress.com/2010/05/.

moving worship experience. Listen – I preach every Sunday in the midst of a wonderful congregation. I've got no problems with a genuine, passionate corporate worship experience. But when we make that the *center* of our life with Christ, instead of seeing it as a celebration of all He's done in us and through us during the rest of the week, we're missing the point! He didn't sit around at the temple, waiting for people to come to Him. He didn't shun the swindlers, whores, and addicts like the rest of society did. He went and ate with them, because that's where light was needed.

With whom are you eating? And I don't mean that as a metaphor: with whom do you spend your time? Where do you spend your time? Jesus said, *"You are the light of the world. A city on a hill cannot be hidden. Neither do people light a lamp and put it under a bowl. Instead they put it on its stand, and it gives light to everyone in the house."* So are you out in the world, shining in the darkness? Or are you hiding under a bowl?

Don't misunderstand; we obviously all must know our limits: men don't need to be "shining their light" inside a strip club, just like recovering alcoholics probably aren't best suited to spend time ministering in the local bars. But when is the last time you purposefully shared a meal with someone whom most of the church would avoid? When is the last time you took the Gospel into a jail? Jesus didn't just ask the people if they had any non-Christian friends. He said, the world is a dark place, and you've got to get out there in it. But let us be clear on this: just *being there* isn't enough.

Let Your Light Shine

In my humble opinion, there is no better American sports movie than *Rudy*. To this day, I find myself pulling for Notre Dame football, for no other reason than for my appreciation of Sean Astin's uplifting portrayal of football's greatest over-achiever.[3] In one of the more compelling story-lines throughout the film, Rudy struggles through difficult relationships with family, teammates and friends. Always discouraging, always doubting, Rudy's closest allies continue to bring a crushing dose of reality to his dream of playing Notre Dame football. So when finally Rudy does make the team, he's overwhelmed with joy. He spends years on the practice squad, his only job to make the starters better, but he doesn't care. He's part of

---

[3] Ease-up, sports fanatics. I'm sure you can think of five people right now who would be considered greater over-achievers in the game of football. That's not really the point, so stay with me here …

the team! But then Rudy's closest confidante on the team offers this one final painful reminder: that's great that you're out there during the week, running practice plays; *but unless you eventually get on that field, for even one play, you'll never be on the record as truly having been a part of this team.*

In the context of the movie, it's a difficult reality to hear; but in the realm of the life of a follower of Jesus, it's a reminder we all need to hear. Understand that I am not here attempting to make a profound statement about grace, salvation, works, or anything like that. I'm simply suggesting that *being in dark places doesn't really amount to much if you're not actively letting your light shine.* Just like a city on a hill, just like a lamp on its stand, "in the same way, let your light shine before men ..." In other words, the purpose of the lamp is not simply *to be* out in the open, but to bring light to the darkness.

"Wow, thanks," you may be thinking. "Who knew that the purpose of light was to illuminate the dark places?" It's true: such an observation seems obvious and hardly worth mentioning. Yet, we too often behave in the world as though this isn't the case. Here is what I mean: we hear instructions about getting out into the world, and then we pat ourselves on the back because, as a matter of fact, we know several people who don't love Jesus. We may even have them over to watch a big game or share coffee. You might have a job in the secular world, where you're around unrepentant sinners all day. So yes, you say, I am truly out in the world! I'm entering into dark places every day!

But let me ask you this: is your presence in those darkened places anything close to true light, making the way clear to those who have been wandering in the dark? Is your life, your conversation, your attitude, your career aspiration, and your decision-making process so unique (read: *unlike the world*) that people are compelled to take notice? You see, we like to imagine that because we affirm certain truths *in our minds*, or because we attend church on [most] Sundays, that we are Christ's ambassadors in a dying world. And yet, what people see is just another person who deals with conflict in the same way, complains about the same things, chases after money and power in the same way. We are not a righteous light in this world simply because of the doctrines to which we cling. We are functioning as light when we proclaim His love with both our *words* and our *actions*.

Words. The apostle Paul once asked, "How, then, can they call on the one they have not believed in? And how can they believe in the one of whom they have not heard? *And how can they hear without someone preaching to them?*" (Romans 10:14, *emphasis mine*). I am not suggesting that your first order of business, as you burst through the doors of the dark places of our culture, is to recite John 3:16 and invite people to say the sinner's prayer. But it is difficult to conceive of a witness to the Good News of Jesus who refuses to open her mouth and speak.

Our fear, of course, is that we'll say the wrong thing. To be precise, many of us are afraid that someone will ask a question or challenge our faith in such a way that we are left without an intelligent response. Guess what: that will probably happen. I wish I could report that loving and following Jesus makes us all intellectual icons, but it doesn't. You're going to run into non-believers who may be deeper thinkers than you. You'll encounter people who have questions that you've either never considered or have not yet resolved in your own mind. And what I want to say to you is, *that's ok.* It's ok to not have all the answers. It's ok to not have a PhD-level mastery of Christian theology. Even if you do, people are always going to question and dispute your doctrines. What they cannot dispute is your story about what Christ has done in you.

When the Lord commissioned His disciples in the first chapter of Acts, He called them to be *witnesses.* Just tell them who I am and what you've seen. Tell them the Good News: that freedom has come through the death and resurrection of Jesus Christ. If your life reflects the truth of your words, and you humbly confess that He has set even a sinner like you free – free to love God and others – there's not going to be much to argue.

Now, with that being said, let me add this: while it doesn't take a seminary degree to bear witness with your words, I do believe we are responsible to be ever-growing in our knowledge of the truth. If the God we worship is not the God of Scripture, we are guilty of idolatry. And as we enter the darkness of the world, those wandering around in it will learn about the nature of God from us. So by all means, start wherever you are and bear witness to Christ – but always strive to know Him more clearly tomorrow than you did today.

Actions. Be intentional about the words you speak. But as the old saying goes, "actions speak louder than words." I once heard it said that there are actually five Gospels: Matthew, Mark, Luke,

John, and the Christian; and much of the world will only ever read the last one. Try to imagine the impact that your lifestyle will have on the world's understanding of Christ. Even if all you have ever told those around you is that you "go to church," their eyes are on you, waiting to see if this Jesus really does make you a new creation, different than you were before.

So what does it mean for your life, your actions, to reflect the light of God? I would argue that such a testimony has to include heavy doses of both *integrity* and *love*. Unfortunately, what we often exhibit in the Church is one or the other. In some circles (particularly in the evangelical world), if we've got one element down, it's integrity (or so we presume). What I mean is, some of us have been raised in a religious culture where we suppose that our greatest impact on the world and on our nation is to denounce the moral evils of our society as loudly as possible. We scream and spit and fight and scratch in the public arena, demanding that the Bible be put back in the courthouse and prayer be put back in the schools. Meanwhile, the Bible is rarely open in our own homes, and prayer is hardly central in the life of our families. What's more, we sing and preach about the matchless grace of Jesus, while exhibiting none of it in the way we engage the world on these issues; thus, we deny the very love we proclaim, even while fighting for the return of Christian principles. In the end, such an approach could hardly be described by the word *integrity*.

Don't get me wrong here: there are some battles worth fighting in our culture. But establishing a moral high ground without love produces little more than legalism, the likes of which Jesus adamantly fought against. That said, over the last several years, one could argue that much of the Church has begun to move in the opposite direction: these days, we often profess love (or so we presume) without modeling integrity. In the wake of the bigger-equals-better mentality of the 80s and 90s, a contingent largely comprised of disenchanted believers has sought a return to the biblical mandate for justice. Very rightly so, the pattern of building bigger buildings with money that could be used to feed the poor (and liberate the oppressed) was challenged. In many ways, such a commitment to genuine Christian principles has led to a healthier understanding of what it means to be the Church.

And yet, many of us became so consumed with separating from our previously legalistic Christian trajectory, that we began to preach love without integrity. We wanted so badly to embrace the broken and the sinful, that we neglected to teach them what it means to obey Christ in every area of our lives. And predictably, this newly distorted commitment began to manifest itself in our lives. Even within the Church, we are often no longer troubled by open rebellion to the Lord. We simply accept worldly lifestyles, fail to lovingly confront sin, just so long as everyone feels welcome and gets along. But what we soon find is that such a willing neglect of sin in the lives of those entering the faith is hardly *loving*. James reminds his readers that "whoever turns a sinner from the error of his way will save him from death and cover over a multitude of sins." Now *that* is love!

If we are really a people who shine light into dark places, we must do so both with our words and our actions. When we think we're bringing light with words only, we are likely only turning people further from the Lord. Nothing is quite so repulsive to a non-believer as a hypocrite: one who claims Jesus but follows the devil. Likewise, if we depend on our actions without a verbal witness, we are really only bringing attention to kindness. Or ourselves. And as Jesus made clear, that misses the point entirely.

Glorifying God

When I was 15 years old, I quickly learned that not every buddy is cut out to be a wingman. The task I gave Jeremy seemed simple enough: go spend a few minutes talking with Marissa, and plow the road for me. Just make small talk, find a way to work me into the conversation, and then promote me like you're Don King. Here in a little bit, I'll head back your way, and then you slide out of the scene like you're invisible. Got it? No problem, he said. I've got your back.

I don't know what "I've got your back" meant in his neighborhood, but clearly it was not the same as in mine. I discovered this about ten minutes after leaving him with the girl of my dreams, when I came back to check on his progress and make my move. As I returned, what I saw was not quite what I had envisioned. To be specific, I saw my "wingman," nuzzling up next to Marissa, laughing and flirting himself into the center ring! After I dealt with the sting of my own missed opportunity, it dawned on me that perhaps he didn't quite understand the concept of a wingman. You see, the wingman's job was to direct attention and glory to another.

Jesus closes out this passage with the following words, pointing to the very purpose of shining light into the darkness: "*that*

38

they may see your good deeds and praise your Father in heaven" (v. 16). Your witness, whether it comes through word or action, through proclamation, purity, or love, is *always* about bringing glory to the Father. If in any sense your light brings praise only to you, you've missed the path that Jesus walked.

In this sense, our lives as light amidst darkness must be considered in even greater depth. For once we recognize that we merely point to something beyond ourselves, we learn that it doesn't suffice to simply go through the motions. Clean living and passionate preaching *alone* don't bring glory to God; rather, His true nature is made known only when these manifestations are the genuine fruit of *love shed abroad in our hearts,* to borrow a phrase from John Wesley. To put it more simply, God is glorified when we get out of the way – when our need for approval, our desire for recognition, and our demand for appreciation are all buried at His feet.

Jesus Himself would later explain why this is true: "I am the light of the world," he said. "Whoever follows me will never walk in darkness, but will have the light of life" (John 8:12). So is He the light, or are we the light? Charles Carter explains this by pointing to the illuminating capacity of the moon.[4] The moon, he notes, sheds light all throughout the darkness of night; yet, the moon itself does not generate light. Rather, it merely reflects the light of the sun, which is the one true source of light. In the same way, as we follow Jesus, we never walk in darkness. He is indeed the light of the world, and those who walk in His steps are enabled to see clearly and bask in its warmth.

But we don't just see this light out in front of us; Jesus said that we will *have* the very light of life. We will possess it, holding it deep within ourselves.[5] So first, our light must point to God, because we are merely reflecting the light of His Son. But secondly – and this is what we must understand – the light we have is not something we can work harder to muster up. We don't go into dark places and just crank out wattage with our heroic efforts. Jesus simply taught that if we're walking with Him, we will have that light in us. We'll be reflecting His light, because His Spirit dwells in us. It's a liberating concept, in that I realize that He is not just sending me to dark places, prodding me to talk about Him. Instead, he extends His hand to me,

---

[4] Carter, p. 32.

[5] This word "have" is translated from the Greek word ἔχω, which means "to have or hold," signifying possession.

and says "Follow me": do what I do, walk how I walk, and you, too, can bring light to the darkest places.

It's a beautiful picture. Still, some will object, arguing that such a commission is for a select group of believers. We hear of opportunities to go on the mission field, bring the Gospel into the prisons, or serve in the homeless shelters and food kitchens, and we slide under our bowls, reasoning to ourselves (and others), "well, I'm not sure God's called *me* to *that*." But such a statement only betrays our misunderstanding of what it means to follow. If He's called you to follow Him,[6] He has called you into the darkest places – the places where sin and brokenness, addiction and shame oppress God's beloved creations. To suggest that He's reserved those fields for another is to deny His Spirit in you.

William Booth puts it more bluntly:

'Not called!' did you say? 'Not heard the call,' I think you should say. Put your ear down to the Bible, and hear him bid you go and pull sinners out of the fire of sin. Put your ear down to the burdened, agonized heart of humanity, and listen to its pitiful wail for help. Go stand by the gates of hell, and hear the damned entreat you to go to their father's house and bid their brothers and sisters, and servants and masters not to come there. And then look Christ in the face, whose mercy you have professed to obey, and tell Him whether you will join heart and soul and body and circumstances in the march to publish His mercy to the world.[7]

His call on you is certain. His promise is sure. He will not send you where He Himself is not. And so, we need not fear the darkness, because our Jesus is there. So go in obedience, enter the depths in faith, because His light dwells in you. It's just like I always tell my children: there's no reason to fear the dark; all you have to do is turn on the light.

Practical Action Step

So how do we put flesh on these bones? I imagine that you're either very excited or incredibly scared right now. It's not easy

---

[6] And He has … I'm hoping this is clear by now.
[7] As quoted by Friedeman, M. (2010). *Discipleship in the Home: Teaching Children, Changing Lives.* Wilmore, KY: Francis Asbury Society, p. 162.

entering the dark places, particularly if we're not accustomed to it. So first, let me suggest this: don't go alone. When Jesus said that "you are the light of the world," He was speaking in the plural. So wherever you go, go together. As for *where* you go, ask the Lord today to give you a burden for a people. In my own church, He has led several of us to take part in a regular ministry with the residents at a local correctional facility. If possible, you could start by taking part in a ministry facilitated through your local church. If such an approach is not available in your setting, take a Christian friend and step out in faith. Visit an inmate, volunteer to tutor children in a local school system. Invite your unsaved neighbors over for dinner. The opportunities are endless.

But as you go, remember these two things: 1) just being there is not the same as letting your light shine. Live in such a way that you bring glory to God, and speak His name as He leads you. 2) This is not a one-time assignment. Flipping a switch on and off again quickly is not the same as illuminating a room. Whatever the Lord leads you to do in this regard, *make it a habit.*

Knowing His Pain

"Follow me."

The original disciples of Jesus weren't the only ones ever to hear that invitation; it was extended to me once too, on the cusp of the Honduran jungle in the middle of the summer. I was 15 years old, experiencing my first few days on the mission field. My church had joined with another local congregation to serve ten days at a boys' school in Honduras; and, as part of our initial weekend onsite, the missionaries decided to take us on a hike through the jungle. The destination sounded incredibly exciting: we were going to work our way through the country until we came upon the caves. They described it as a fascinating series of rock formations, through which we could hike, explore, and even race down a mudslide. You've never seen anything like it, they told us!

"So, follow me," our leader said. And I did, with enthusiasm! I loved the idea of exploring caves in a remote part of the world. I was on an adventure, and so a hike through the jungle actually sounded kind of fun. But then we started hiking ... through the jungle. Did I mention it was July? To be honest, the first part wasn't so bad. About 30 of us were walking through the lush, green landscape – following trails and walking along streams. Every now and then, we'd jump over rocks or fallen trees; it was a rough path, but in a fun way, if you like to hike.

When we hit the half-hour mark, I decided to follow the missionary kids as they veered off the trail a bit. I was in the back of the line, behind them, so I didn't think much of it. We were separated from the larger group for maybe five to ten minutes, but we found a place to drink from a freshwater stream, and we explored for a few minutes in a denser part of the jungle. I was having a blast – until we rejoined the group, and I saw my youth pastor coming. Maybe he wanted to hear about my adventure! That notion quickly dissipated when he grabbed ahold of my shirt, pulled me close, and quietly[8] made clear the importance of sticking with the group. Oops. Now he was mad and I was discouraged.

Once we'd been walking for about an hour, I wondered if I was going to ever see a cave. A few minutes later, I wondered if I cared whether or not I ever saw a cave. At the 90 minute mark, I thought about asking how close we were, but I was one of the younger guys on the trip, and I didn't want to look like a baby. As time went on, my legs grew sore, I was sweating in strange places, and I must have been bitten by a thousand mosquitos. I was tired and miserable, and there was no end in sight! I was in the back of the line, I'd been chewed out by my leader, and everyone else looked like they were having a blast. Few times in my life can I remember ever having felt so alone. What started off as a grand adventure soon became a march of misery, as the journey was now awfully tough. I hadn't really seen this coming when we first started out, and all I could think was, *this isn't what I signed on for.*

Peter felt the warm blood trickling down his back. As he knelt there, hunched over, all he could see were blurry faces. He hadn't meant to cry, but the pain alone had caused his eyes to water. And now, as he tried to look up, he could only see the general form of his accusers. As the whip struck him again, he heard a gasp slip out of his mouth, from somewhere deep in his chest. The pain was so intense that he could barely control his own voice. Each time it struck his flesh, he could feel it tearing; but perhaps the worst part was the anticipation. He could hear the air whistle ever-so-slightly as the whip drew back to strike him again.

As he endured the painful abuse, his mind began to wander back to that day at the lake. "Follow me," Jesus had said, "and I will make you fishers of men." He'd never even thought about doing anything else. Everyone in his family was a fisherman – it wasn't like it was making him wealthy, but he had a pretty good life. But then this strange man came along and offered him an adventure. *Follow*

---

[8] Not the gentle, soft-spoken type of *quietly*, but the "I'd-end-your-life-if-we-were-alone-in-the-jungle" kind. My mom used to whisper like that when we were in trouble – it's terrifying. For what it's worth, I tried that with my kids, but they just kept asking me to speak up. I guess we all have our gifts, and mine do not include the crazy-whisper to children.

me, and I'll do something even greater with your life. Follow me, and together we'll do something the world has never seen. As Peter's mind drifted back to that critical day, he remembered the exhilaration of jumping off that boat. He'd never felt so alive! He was going to do great things!

Crack! The whip struck him again. The pain was so acute, Peter worried for a moment that he might actually vomit. It hurt all the way through to his stomach. He had no idea how many blows had been delivered now. Would it end soon? His thoughts wandered once again. This time, he recalled what it was like to stand up before that crowd in Jerusalem not long ago. Who would have ever thought that so many people would be interested in anything he had to say? But there he was, standing in front of Jews from all over the world! The funny thing is, he wasn't even nervous. He could feel a certainty, a power, rising up within Him – not the power of macho confidence, but a surge of love, wisdom, and inner strength. The Spirit of the Lord was upon him, and he knew it.

So he just spoke the truth. He wasn't quite sure where the words came from, but even he could sense their power. When he finished his speech, these faces, which were once angry and derisive, were now just pitiable. When some asked, "What should we do?" Peter remembered not hesitating for a second: "Repent and be baptized, every one of you, in the name of Jesus Christ ..."[9] And so they did. Three thousand of them! Jesus was right! He had indeed sent the Counselor to remain with us! I was His witness on that day! The adventure was playing out just as He had described.

Crack! That final blow was the most painful; in fact, it was the very pain of it that ushered his thoughts back to his present reality. He turned to his left and saw James slumped over on the ground, Peter finally got an indication of what his own back probably looked like. He realized that they were going to have to help each other walk out. As he and his friends began to gather one another up, Peter couldn't help but wonder if it was all worth it. Is this what Jesus meant all those times He talked about adventure? Is this what it would look like to be *fishers of men*? Was their current suffering going to be the norm? Given the religious and cultural climate, he didn't see any other way.

As the weight of that realization began to sink in, Peter remembered another day – a more somber day. Jesus, more and

---

[9] Acts 2:38.

more, had been talking about His own departure. His friends didn't quite understand all of what He told them, but they knew it wasn't good. It was clear that Jesus was going to have to suffer. But then He said this:

> *If the world hates you, keep in mind that it hated me first. If you belonged to the world, it would love you as its own. As it is, you do not belong to the world, but I have chosen you out of the world. That is why the world hates you. Remember the words I spoke to you: 'No servant is greater than his master.' If they persecuted me, they will persecute you also. If they obeyed my teaching, they will obey yours also. They will treat you this way because of my name, for they do not know the One who sent me. If I had not come and spoken to them, they would not be guilty of sin. Now, however, they have no excuse for their sin. He who hates me hates my Father as well. If I had not done among them what no one else did, they would not be guilty of sin. But now they have seen these miracles, and yet they have hated both me and my Father. But this is to fulfill what is written in their Law: 'They hated me without reason.' When the Counselor comes, whom I will send to you from the Father, the Spirit of truth who goes out from the Father, he will testify about me. And you also must testify, for you have been with me from the beginning. All this I have told you so that you will not go astray. They will put you out of the synagogue; in fact, a time is coming when anyone who kills you will think he is offering a service to God. They will do such things because they have not known the Father or me. I have told you this, so that when the time comes you will remember that I warned you. I did not tell you this at first because I was with you."*
> *(John 15:18 – 16:4)*

As Peter pondered over those words, a smile slowly crept over his face. As he looked over at John, it appeared that the same realization was dawning on him as well. Without any other words spoken between them, it was as if all of them understood the same truth at the same moment: this painful beating was not a setback to the path of Jesus – this *was* the path! In fact, this was precisely how He'd said it would go for us if we followed Him. He said we'd have to lose to win. He said we'd have to be last to be first. He said we'd have to take up our own cross daily to follow Him! And in an instant,

45

their grief turned to joy. *"The apostles left the Sanhedrin, rejoicing because they had been counted worthy of suffering disgrace for the Name."*[10]

That last verse has always been a hard pill for me to swallow. I could live with something like, "They didn't reject the Lord because they'd suffered for the Name;" or, I could even reconcile "They eventually saw the long-term value in suffering for the Name." But *rejoicing*? Right as they were leaving, while the blood was still flowing? Is that even realistic? The reason that perhaps many of us are asking questions like this is because we have likely experienced our own form of suffering as followers of Christ. For most of us, at some point, the harsh reality of experience reveals to us that our walk with Christ is not going to be all adrenaline-pumping adventure.

Like the disciples, there has been painted for us a spectacular picture of the finish line: we will eventually enter into His glorious presence for all of eternity. Even in this life, we will experience fulfillment, joy, and the reward of making disciples and shining His light into the dark places of the world. And for all who have submitted themselves to Christ, all who have walked in obedience and experienced the joy of being part of the rescue mission, we know that this is no false advertising. Walking with Him is incredibly fulfilling and electrifying. And yet, what we also soon discover is that this path isn't always exciting. Sometimes the road gets rough. Sometimes we sweat, we bleed, we get bit, we experience loneliness; and for many believers around the world today, we endure the torture of first-century-style persecution.

The cold, hard truth of discipleship is this: *to follow Jesus is to willingly enter the road of suffering.* Our Lord neither sugar-coated that fact, nor did He hide it from His followers. He said, "If they persecuted me," (and they did), "they will persecute you also" (they either are, or they will). And so if we believe this, I can't help but wonder how we ever get to the place where, like the apostles, we are able to *rejoice* in it. How do we come to the point where we celebrate in affliction, because we too were counted worthy to suffer for the Name?

---

[10] Acts 5:41.

46

Answering that question is the goal of this chapter. That said, let us start with this caveat: most of us will be hard-pressed to go out and *seek out* suffering for the Lord. Unlike some of the other issues we've explored, suffering is not something we can very easily *go do* for Him. But, what we can do is prepare ourselves for the persecution about which our Master has warned us. What we can do is learn to embrace such pain as an integral part of our lives as His followers – so that when suffering does come, we not only refuse to be discouraged, but that we are able, like the apostles, to truly rejoice in Him. So how do we do that? I would suggest that the place to begin is by exploring these critical questions: *what* is suffering? *Why* do we suffer? *Where* will we suffer? And, *how* should we suffer?

The What

If we are to engage in any meaningful discourse about suffering for the sake of Christ, we must first come to an agreement about what persecution really is. I would submit that this is no easy task, because I often struggle to settle in my *own* mind what qualifies as persecution today, much less trying to agree on a definition with another person. So where do we begin? Let us first explore our options.

On the one hand, there are many days when I am firmly convinced that what most North Americans endure today cannot conceivably be described as persecution. For instance, consider the account of the Roman historian Tacitus, reporting on the treatment of Christians in the first century under the rule of Nero:

> *Before killing the Christians, Nero used them to amuse the people. Some were dressed in furs, to be killed by dogs. Others were crucified. Still others were set on fire early in the night, so that they might illumine it. Nero opened his own gardens for these shows ...*[11]

Justo Gonzalez adds that it was under Nero that both Peter and Paul were likely martyred.[12] What's more, such abuse is not merely limited to the annals of Christian history. Even during the past year in China, Christian church leaders have seen their churches forcibly

---

[11] As quoted by Gonzalez, J. (1984). *The Story of Christianity, Vol. 1: The Early Church to the Dawn of the Reformation.* New York, NY: HarperCollins, p. 35.
[12] Gonzalez, p. 35.

sealed up, as they themselves were detained and sent to labor camps by their own government.[13] So, when I hear about an American Christian who is merely made to be the butt of a joke because she carries a Bible to school or to work? That's a bummer, but ... *please*.

On the other hand, there are days when I am reminded that persecution will look different in different cultures. What's more, physical violence is not the only legitimate form of torture. I have been overwhelmed of late, as I've heard story after story (even locally) of teenagers committing suicide because they had been bullied at school.[14] One 12-yr-old boy in our community was abused so mercilessly by his peers that he recently hung himself in his own closet, while his father and brother were making dinner in the next room. In light of this, it is difficult to argue that even being teased by others for the faith we proclaim is not a form of persecution. Just because we do not walk away with broken bones or bloodied faces does not mean that we are not suffering for the Name. It's true, most of us reading these pages are not currently in danger of imprisonment or beatings from our government. But was the warning of Jesus limited to such a specific form of abuse?

So which option is most accurate? What does it mean to be persecuted for our faith? Ought we be incredibly selective with our use of the *p*-word? Or can ordinary citizens of a free nation like the U.S.A. also face real forms of suffering for the Name of Jesus? I don't know that we'll get to the place where we all agree – for that matter, I don't know that I'll get to the place where I am certain of my own opinion. But for the sake of the ensuing discussion, I will adopt a broader view of suffering; because, in the end, I am ill-equipped to determine for another believer what qualifies as suffering. So let us agree, at least for the time being, that persecution (in the context of Christianity) is defined as *any form of abuse inflicted on a follower of Christ, as a result of his or her witness.*

The Why

While I intend to proceed with such a definition *cautiously*, I will also do so *intentionally*. What I mean is, consider the implication

---

[13] See http://www.christianpost.com/news/christian-persecution-in-china-rises-over-40-percent-in-2012-chinaaid-reports-89542/.

[14] The NIMH asserts that in 2007, suicide was the third-leading cause of death for young people, ages 15-24. See http://www.nimh.nih.gov/health/publications/suicide-in-the-us-statistics-and-prevention/index.shtml.

of the final segment: *as a result of his or her witness.* The fact is, all of us are going to experience hardship and suffering in this life. Despite what you may hear from some of the well-groomed preachers on television, becoming a Christian is no ticket to an easy life. You still may have financial difficulties. You still may get the flu. People in your life will still pass away, sometimes under tragic circumstances. Accepting the Lord's invitation to follow Him does not mean that you will never lose your job, lose your home, or find yourself in a crumbling relationship.

Suffering can come our way for several reasons. Sometimes, we suffer because we've made terrible decisions. Whether it was a choice made before or after our conversion, we must recognize that *our own sin* leads to many of the trials we face. It could be that you are losing your job, not because you are being persecuted for your faith, but because you were rude to customers and you kept lying about being sick. It could be that your colleagues are stand-offish at work, not because you go to church, but because you talk about them behind their backs. Many times, when we suffer, we need to first examine whether or not it is coming as a consequence of sin in our lives, past or present.

In other instances, our suffering simply serves as a reminder of our dependence on the Lord. Paul wrote to the Corinthians about what he referred to as *a thorn in his flesh* (2 Cor. 12:7). He said, I begged the Lord three different times to take it away from me, but He would not do it! Instead, God reminded Paul that His grace alone was sufficient. He reminded Paul that such trials create an environment for God's power to be perfected in our lives through our very weakness. In this case, it neither appears that Paul was actively sinning, nor would the context suggest that he was experiencing persecution. Rather, his suffering was being used of God to bring him into a fuller maturity of faith.

We can see, then, that suffering and trials can derive from various sources. Yet, the persecution Jesus warned about in the Gospel of John was of a very particular sort. The world will hate you, He said, *because you do not belong to them.* The early church quickly discovered that their allegiance to Jesus separated them from many other Jews and Gentiles alike. Despite the earliest Christians' conviction that their faith was the true fulfillment of Judaism, many faithful Jews regarded these disciples' claims as heresy against God.[15]

---

[15] Gonzalez, pp. 20, 32.

As the divide grew between Christianity and Judaism, the number of Christians was growing at the same time. Now comprising a considerable segment of society, the Christians soon attracted the attention of the Romans as well. And while it is clear that some of the persecution they faced from the State was a result of individual cruelty (read: *Nero*), much of the animosity towards them derived from the common Roman belief that they genuinely hated mankind.[16]

How could such a charge be made? Primarily, the problem was that the Christians refused to participate in many of the staples of Roman culture. As Gonzalez notes, "all social activities – the theatre, the army, letters, sports – were so entwined with pagan worship that Christians often felt the need to abstain from them."[17] Therefore, all those faithful Romans who were passionate about their society, offering their allegiance to *culture*, viewed the Christians as, ironically, *ir*religious. The early Christians were hated because they did not belong to the world – they did not pursue the same activities, worship the same gods, or live their lives in the same way that the rest of the world did. Instead, they belonged to Jesus.

Can we pause for a moment and ask ourselves this question: does the world hate us because we're different? Are you despised by the world because you refuse to chase money and promotions the same way they do? Are you scorned by your culture, because you refuse to turn your sexuality into a bargaining chip, or because you decline to allow the current trend of cultural "morality" to dictate what you affirm as right or wrong? Or, do they just hate you because you're hateful and judgmental? *Or*, do they not hate you at all? Here's my point – actually, there are two, and the first one is this: being hated because we do not belong to the world *is not the same* as being hated because we fail to love others as Jesus has loved.

I cringe whenever I see professing Christians angrily picketing[18] against the depravity of society, red-faced and screaming about how much God hates sinners. I cringe because these are often the first ones lamenting their status as victims of religious

---

[16] Tacitus is quoted by Gonzalez (p. 35) as saying that the Christians were punished "for their hatred of humankind."

[17] Ibid.

[18] Am I suggesting that all forms of public demonstration are unloving? No. Surely there are instances in our society when we must stand up for the voiceless victims of our world. But in all such instances, we must be directed by love – both for God and for humanity.

persecution, hated by a godless society. "They hate us because of our faith!" No, they hate you because you're a jerk. Your refusal to show love, particularly to the absolute worst of humanity, does not make you anything like Jesus. When we are despised less for our beliefs and more for our attitudes towards those who disagree with us, we are not facing the type of persecution which Jesus described.

Secondly, we must be reminded that followers of Jesus will be persecuted for our *testimony*, not simply for what we *think* about Jesus. Drawing from the report of Tacitus once more, it is significant that he noted that the reason for the arrest of the Christians was due to their *confession*; and the further condemnation of others came on the basis of their *testimony*.[19] That is to say, no one was ever persecuted simply because they "believed in their heart." Rather, the suffering was inflicted because Christians claimed the Lordship of Christ – through verbal testimony, as well as through the way they lived. Jesus was clear on this point as well, when He noted that "[his followers] must testify, for you have been with me from the beginning" (John 15:27). The expectation was that His people would be testifying about Him – not simply affirming doctrines internally.

The significance for you and me, then, is this: we cannot claim religious persecution if we are not bearing witness to the Resurrection of Christ, both with our words and with our lives. If we are not truly set apart from the ways of this world, then we are not experiencing the hatred that Jesus did. You will be persecuted, He said, "because of my name" (v. 21). Does the world even hear His name from you?

The Where

Up to this point, I have been examining the type of persecution that comes from *the world*. Jesus used this phrase to refer to the non-believing society which existed all around His followers. But as He later noted, this would not be the only source of suffering for the Christians:

> All this I have told you so that you will not go astray. They will put you out of the synagogue; in fact, a time is coming when anyone who kills you will think he is offering a service to God. They will do such things because they have not known the Father or me (John 16:1-3).

---

[19] Gonzalez, p. 35.

Without question, Jesus declared to His disciples that the world would hate and abuse them because of His name. But we must not miss His staggering statement that *even those professing to be God's children would reject them*. Think about it for a moment from their perspective: the synagogue was all they'd known up to this point. For His original listeners, to be faithful to God was to be obedient to the Law and to be a part of the community of the synagogue. The truth was, they were accustomed to abuse from the nations; these men in particular had spent their entire lives under the thumb of the Roman Empire. But what Jesus said in this moment must have been a shock to their system: even our own people – God's elect – will cast us out?

Church history abounds with stories of the Roman persecution of Christians; but when we examine the book of Acts, we see that the first persecutors of the believers were the religious leaders of the synagogues. Up until the days of Jesus, these were the men whom were counted upon to lead people into a right relationship with the Lord. It would surely be naïve to suggest that Jesus completely transformed people's opinions of these leaders during His public ministry – chances are, the hypocrisy and elitism of the Pharisees, for instance, were already easily observed by the common folk. Nevertheless, Jesus was now stating emphatically that to follow Him would even cost His disciples their standing within the established religion. And for a people whose very identity was grounded in this religion, this was no small matter.

So how does this warning translate for us? First, as it has already been established, we must expect to suffer at the hands of an unbelieving world. Obviously, the majority of this passage speaks directly to that. But secondly, I would argue that we must also be prepared to face rejection even in the local church.

During my days in youth ministry, I remember the pain on the face of one of my students as she recounted her experience from the night before. A student at a Christian high school, this young lady had spent years with many of her classmates, studying the Scripture in class, praising the Lord in chapel services, and even serving together in the community. She wasn't idealistic about their sincerity – she knew that not everyone in a Christian school was necessarily a Christian – but she was rather certain that many of them really did love Jesus.

However, her heart was broken as she shared with me about what had gone on at the home of one of her classmates the night before. Granted, it wasn't anything illegal; but the conversations, the choice of entertainment, and the general atmosphere were nothing different than what she would have expected in the secular world. As she expressed her concern to others, she was made to feel like an outcast even among believers, derided for her "radical" principles. She was nearly in tears as she described her pain over that sort of isolation from people she believed to be disciples of Christ.

It would be easy to dismissively suggest that her friends really weren't Christians after all. Perhaps that is true in some cases. But the crucial reality which we must come to understand is that, unfortunately, the *Church* [big C] is not always the same as the *church* [little c].[20] What I mean is this: our local churches are filled with people, some of whom are disciples, and some of whom are not. I do not say this as an invitation for all of us to go sort out which is which; rather, I offer it simply as a reminder. If we set our mark no higher than the body of professing believers, when it comes to our measure of what is *normal* in terms of both morality and standard of faith, we're likely going to find ourselves disappointed. In fact, if we are genuinely following Jesus wherever He goes (particularly into the dark places), we may even face abuse, isolation and rejection from others who claim to follow Him. That is why we must continue to hold *Christ* as our standard of obedience (not other people), regardless of how others respond.

Does this mean we're free to ignore the church and "go where the Lord leads" us as individuals? Far from it. We were made for community, and we can only reflect His full image in the context of the church. We *need* one another to follow Him. But we must also recognize that the local church (little c) is not immune to the same problem which plagued much of the leadership of the Jewish synagogues: "they have not known the Father or me." I believe His warning, translated to our context, is not a free pass to disregard the local church. Rather, it is simply a call to prepare yourself even for persecution from sources you may not anticipate. It hurts

---

[20] I'm here attempting to distinguish between those who are truly part of the body of Christ – *big C* Church, the Church universal – from the group of people meeting with you on Sunday (*little c* church). This is not meant as an attack on the local church, which I both adore and highly value. Too many Christians these days seem to prefer to attack the local church than to participate in its edification – this is a tendency I desperately want to avoid.

profoundly when we are injured by those who profess Christ. But then again, our Lord never promised freedom from pain.

The How

While it is enormously helpful to gain insight into the *why*'s and *where*'s of persecution, we still must come face-to-face with the practical application of it. In other words, exactly *how are we supposed to endure this type of suffering*? Given the breadth of his own experience, I find it particularly illuminating to return to Peter. In his first letter, written to the persecuted Christians spread across northern Asia Minor, he offers a treasure trove of insight into how to endure suffering for the Name of Christ. My best advice would be to read the letter in its entirety. But for the purposes of this chapter, allow me to share two significant highlights:

"But in your hearts, set apart Christ as Lord" (1 Peter 3:15).

Peter offers this admonition in conjunction with an encouragement to refuse to fear the threats of our persecutors. Regardless of the trials we face for the Name of Christ, we must take comfort in the reality that He is Lord. Not only does He exercise all power over our circumstances, our accusers, and our fate; but, He is also the Master of our attitudes and reactions. And let us not forget, this is meant to be a *developed attitude of submission*. We would all love to convince ourselves that, in the moment of martyrdom, with the gun to our head, so to speak, we would boldly confess the name of Jesus. Sadly, most of us fail that test often, with no more pressure than a tempting alternative, or the threat of awkwardness in a relationship. What I mean is, most of us are not being forced to choose between Christ and the world in life-threatening situations. But we do make that choice daily with what we elect to pursue in this life, and in the ways we treat and respond to people. Do you really think that if you're not setting Him apart as Lord of all your ways *now*, you'd step up and praise Him when your life was on the line?

In my opinion ... that's unlikely. So rather than praying for miraculous assistance if and when you're ever "put to the test," why not assess your life now? Why not begin practicing the presence of the Lord this day, laying before Him every desire of your heart? Peter describes this way of life as being prepared to give a reason for the hope you have, learning to do this with love and respect, and always keeping a clear conscience.

54

"When they hurled their insults at him, he did not retaliate; when he suffered, he made no threats. Instead, he entrusted himself to him who judges justly" (1 Peter 2:23). Secondly, Peter points to the example of Jesus, when He suffered for our sins. Rather than answering every accusation, rather than fighting to defend His reputation, He simply trusted the Father to vindicate Him. Is this how you live your life? I get all bent out of shape when someone tells me I'm too sensitive ("how dare you suggest that I am easily offended?! That ... offends me!"). Most of us are so consumed with pride and are so protective of our reputations, that we would sooner fight for a positive public image for ourselves, than we would for the protection of the defenseless people of this world. Peter said, when you face persecution, let the Lord prove your righteousness.

Admittedly, this is easier said than done. Few of us can easily stomach false accusations and unjust abuse; but, think of it this way: in whose hands is your reputation the safest? Do you truly believe that He can be trusted to vindicate your character? That He can be trusted to carry you through whatever abuses are thrust upon you? Ultimately, we have not been called to retaliate or to whisper threats of our own in the midst of such trials; instead, our instructions are to love our enemies, to pray for those who persecute us (Matthew 5:44), and to willingly suffer for doing good. For, *"to this you were called, because*

> *Christ suffered for you, leaving you an example, that you should follow in his steps"* (1 Peter 2:21).

Practical Action Step

Again, as I indicated above, we can't exactly go outside today and choose to be persecuted. So what do we do? Perhaps our best guide is to follow the steps outlined by Peter: first, set apart Christ as Lord in your life. Maybe that means making an assessment of your ambitions in life. Maybe it means being honest with yourself about how you treat people, the entertainment you choose, and how you make decisions in general: is He truly Lord? If not, confess to Him the areas He does not currently rule, and ask Him to take over. Secondly, if you are facing any backlash today for your faith, cease any and all retaliation. Set aside your self-defense, and focus your attention on the testimony of your life. See to it that you are living an honorable life – in every way – and entrust your reputation to the Lord.

Finally, we must be reminded that the hatred of the world is reserved for those who testify to the Name of Jesus. Surely, it *matters* what we believe in our hearts; but, our Lord has called us to testify to what we've seen. If you long "to know Christ and the power of his resurrection and *the fellowship of sharing in his sufferings*" (Phil. 3:10, *emphasis mine*), then seek out an opportunity to testify to the world. Whether it reaches to the masses or just to one neighbor, they need to hear His name from you.

Your Turn

"3-2-1-Fly! ... Fly!" They weren't supposed to have to say it twice. But, frankly, it was my hand on the rip cord, and I was going to pull it when I was good and ready. When you're dangling 170 feet in the air, with nothing between you and the ground but a bungee cord and an apron, you've earned the right to call the shots. At least that's my opinion.

Less than one year before stepping off that bridge on the back roads of Kentucky, I was dangling from a tower somewhere near Cincinnati, Ohio with my two best friends. We'd decided to pay the extra cash and take on our greatest fear: bungee jumping. To be precise, it wasn't so much bungee *jumping*, as it was bungee *falling*. The idea behind this extreme amusement park ride was simple: they put you on a big platform with two friends and have you each put on a super-apron.[1] Then, they attach a giant bungee cord to the back of all three of you and instruct you to just lean forward in the apron. Next, the platform beneath your feet lowers, and there you are, dangling about 12 feet in the air. That's when the real terror begins.

Slowly and steadily, as my friends and I were now in a horizontal position, side-by-side with our stomachs to the ground, the cord behind us drew us up into the air towards the tower above. Somewhere around 30-40 feet, I could feel my body clenching up. But we were all 18 years old at the time, full of male bravado, and so any expression of fear had to be masked in the form of a nervous joke. Suddenly, I was Jerry Seinfeld in a super-apron. After what felt like several minutes, I assumed we must have just about reached the peak of our ascent. To confirm, I twisted my head around to take a look at the tower above me. Imagine my horror when I realized that

---

[1] This is what I told myself, anyway. I mean, if it's not a *super*-apron, then trusting it to keep you from certain death is pretty foolish, right? Super-apron, it is!

we were only about half-way up. Suddenly, awkward jokes were no longer sufficient to mask the fear; thus, I gave up the funnies and went to a mixture of silence and slow Lamaze breathing.[2]

By the time we finally reached the top, I could barely speak, even if I had wanted to. Only from the relative security of an airplane or a building had I ever seen the earth from this high up. Somehow, I had been granted the position of rip-cord-guy, and the job was simple, they said. When you get to the top, we'll say, "3-2-1, Fly!" When you hear that, just pull the rip cord and you'll embark on the ride of your life! Easy, right? The only problem was, at 170 feet, I discovered that my muscles didn't respond to instruction in the same way they did on the ground. So there we were, suspended in the air with dozens of people below waiting on me to act. Only, it wasn't happening. And in my hesitation, I found the time to ask myself this question: *what if we just stayed here, like this?* Wouldn't that be strange? We'd paid the money, we'd donned our super-aprons, and we took the time to be drawn up into the sky. What if I just *never* pulled this cord?

Coming off what could only be described as a disappointing trip to His hometown (more on this later), Jesus headed out into the nearby villages to teach and to minister to the people. While such a venture was nothing new – after all, this had been His pattern from the beginning of His public ministry (e.g., see Mark 1:38-39) – his *strategy* this time would prove to be a bit different:

> *Calling the Twelve to him, he sent them out two by two and gave them authority over evil spirits. These were his instructions: "Take nothing for the journey except a staff – no bread, no bag, no money in your belts. Wear sandals but not an extra tunic. Whenever you enter a house, stay there until you leave that town. And if any place will not welcome you or listen to you, shake the dust off your feet when you leave, as a testimony against them." They went out and preached that people should repent. They drove out many demons and*

---

[2] For the record, my wife doesn't find this reference funny. In fact, any time I compare my own life struggles to giving birth (a feat which she has nobly accomplished twice), *it's not funny.*

anointed many sick people with oil and healed them. (Mark 6:7-13)

While we are here given a sufficient account of what these men were *told* – as well as what they ultimately *did* – what is missing is any commentary on how they *felt* about this stunning commission. Can you imagine what this must have been like for them? What questions, thoughts, and fears must have been bouncing through their minds? Given all they'd seen Jesus do during the course of their time together, was He really sitting here telling them that they were going to now go out and do the same? Preach like Him, heal like Him, cast out demons like Him? Had He lost His mind?!

A few months after our bungee incident, I spent a week at the beach with those same friends. One memorable evening, we took a trip to a chain restaurant where, much to our delight, an illusionist was performing little tricks as he moved from table to table.[3] As he made his way to our section, it was all I could do to stifle my exuberance; I couldn't wait to see what he was going to do! And I mean to tell you, the strange little man delivered. He put a single red clown nose in his hand, had me tap it, and suddenly there were two. He took a dollar bill from one of my friends, had us write on it, and then made it dance in mid-air, not two feet from my face. We laughed and cheered so rigorously that one of my buddies nearly choked to death[4] on a French fry.[5] We loved this man's performance, because right before our very eyes, he was performing acts that defied logic. He was doing things right in our midst which we couldn't explain!

Imagine, then, if a handful of young men in the 1990's were giddy over a reproducing clown nose and a flying dollar bill, what a dozen young men in the first century must have thought about all they'd seen from Jesus. In the previous chapter alone, Mark describes a scene witnessed by three of them, where the Lord literally spoke to a dead girl and told her to get up (Mark 5:41)! She

---

[3] Confession time: I love this form of entertainment. I don't care that it's simply a matter of sleight-of-hand and optical illusions – I just very much enjoy being amazed by the unexplainable … or at least the difficult-to-explain.

[4] True story. This was actually quite traumatic for us all … for at least 90 seconds. Because, when you're 18, it never takes long before your buddy's trauma turns into just another joke at the table.

[5] Or a *freedom* fry? Are we still doing that?

was totally gone, the family was in mourning, and Jesus just took her hand and said, "Little girl, I say to you, get up!" And she did! Talk about fry-choking-awe! Most of us cannot begin to fathom the experience of standing right next to Jesus as He made miracles happen in the villages ... let alone being called into a meeting where He told us, "Now it's your turn. You're going to go out and do what I've been doing."

Thus far, following Jesus has proven to be quite an adventure for these disciples. Walking in His steps has called not only for a transformation of their beliefs, but for a full commitment of their lives. They've jumped off their boats, into the unknown; they've been called upon to follow Him into the darkness, to forgive others, and have embarked on the road of suffering with Jesus. So far, they've been watching and learning and following; but now, the Lord has invited them to do the impossible. Now, He has looked them in the eyes and said, *it's your turn*. In that moment, the disciples were called upon to move from the role of observers into full participation. *Following Jesus would require that they accept the commission to reproduce His ministry.* Given all they'd seen, it must have seemed like an impossible assignment. So how is it that they met the challenge?

That is what we will explore together in this chapter. We'll examine what He called them to do, how He sent them to do it, and what would be necessary for their success. In so doing, my hope is that we will better understand the invitation that is likewise extended to us today: that following Jesus still requires us to get up off the sidelines and do the impossible.

Extending His Ministry

On its face, the assignment He gave them was ridiculous: this collection of fishermen (along with a tax collector and a political activist, to name just a few) was supposed to go from town to town and call Jews to repentance, send demons running, and wipe away sickness and disease with a touch of their hand? These guys weren't educated rabbis. They weren't priests or prophets. They were just regular Joes! They hadn't ever come close to preaching, let alone performing miracles – in fact, some have argued that a few of them may have even been teenagers![6] Why would Jesus send out this seemingly ill-equipped bunch to take on such monumental tasks?

---

[6] http://kbonikowsky.wordpress.com/2008/08/20/jesus-disciples-a-teenage-posse/.

Viewed from that perspective, we may get the sense that Jesus was setting them up for failure. Yet, what we cannot afford to miss is the fact that He was not sending them to do anything which He'd not already been doing Himself. Or to put it another way, Jesus was sending these young men not to chart a new course of kingdom work, but *to serve as an extension of His own ministry*. This needs to be understood from two angles.

First, even in Mark's brief narrative which precedes this passage, consider all that we (and they) have seen Jesus doing. Prior to calling the first disciples, we are informed that "Jesus went into Galilee, proclaiming the good news of God. 'The time has come,' he said. 'The kingdom of God is near. Repent and believe the good news!'" (Mark 1:14-15). The very core of His public ministry was the proclamation of this message – particularly throughout the local villages (Mark 1:38). In the same chapter, He revealed His power by casting out an evil spirit which had possessed a man in the synagogue. He amazed all the people because of His authority – not only as a teacher, but over the spiritual realm as well (Mark 1:21-27). Before the first chapter ends, Jesus not only heals a town full of sick people (1:33-34), but also cleanses a leper from his disease, right on the spot (1:42).

In one chapter, we see Him call Jews to repentance, send demons running, and wipe away sickness and disease with a touch of his hand. Does this sound familiar? Not to mention His healing (physical and spiritual) of a paralytic (ch. 2), His authoritative teaching (chs. 2-4), His silencing of a storm (ch. 4), His victory over a legion of spirits (ch. 5), cleansing of a chronically ill woman (ch. 5), and … wait for it … *His raising of the dead* (ch. 5)! For five straight chapters, this type of ministry is all we've seen from Jesus. So let us be clear: when He calls His disciples to go out and do the same, this was not an assignment out of left field. Effectively, what He was telling them was simple: you know all that you've seen me do, as we have walked together? This has been your training. Now I am sending you to do the same.

Right … *simple*. Listen, I've *seen* several Olympic sprinters run 100 meters in less than ten seconds; it doesn't mean I am ready to go out and do the same. Simply observing a ministry does not enable one to carry it out; but it appears that Jesus was not oblivious to this reality. This is why, secondly, it is critical to note that He not only sent them out to minister, but *He gave them the authority* (v. 7) to do it as well.

In my never-ending quest to maintain[7] the physique of an 18-year-old athlete, I recently obtained a chin-up bar for my house. And every time I set it up and exert myself on this "exercise tool" (read: *torture rack*), my children delight in what they're witnessing. I don't know whether they are experiencing awe or pity by watching me, but either way, they are captivated. So, when I finish a round, I often encourage them to take a turn: an invitation that gets them more excited than just watching, to be sure. Now, over the course of a year or so, they've undoubtedly seen me do ... *tens* of chin-ups. Yet, when I call them over to do some of their own – to continue my exercise routine – I know that I can't simply stand back and tell them to get to it.

First of all, they can't reach the bar. So I pick them up and help them get their hands situated. Then, at least at first, I hold them around the legs, taking some of the weight off their arms. Depending on the child, I may even have to do a little lifting to get them up to where they need to be. Now, when we operate in this way, are my children doing chin-ups? Of course. But they're exercising only in the strength of their dad. To best understand the commissioning of these disciples, I think we are wise to understand their ministry in the same way. They most assuredly went out and did what they'd seen from Jesus; but make no mistake about it, they did not go alone. Their capacity to heal sickness, their authority over the Enemy, and even their power to preach repentance were all sourced in the authority of Jesus Himself. In this way, they were serving as an extension, not only of the *practice* of His ministry, but also the *power*. That being said, this was not the only sense in which the disciples did not go alone.

Two-by-Two

"Sometimes you don't want to do these things by yourself. I got your back." That was the encouragement I received from my buddy Carlton, right before I met up with a former girlfriend to exchange a few items we'd borrowed from one another. That's always a fun meeting. And in this case, I had even greater reason for trepidation, as this was no cordial break-up. Sadly, this teenage relationship ended on quite a sour note, with neither of us venturing to offer the classic suggestion, "let's still be friends." That wasn't exactly on the table at this point. So as I prepared myself for our

---

[7] Come to think of it, I guess the word *maintain* implies that such a level of fitness and strength was once mine. How about *acquire*? That's better.

final meeting, I didn't quite know what to expect; but my buddy felt it was better to take no chances. "I'll just be there with you, sort of roaming in the background." Given my aversion to conflict, that sounded pretty good to me. As it turned out, the exchange was very calm, and even somewhat friendly. In hindsight, it could have been partly due to my friend's decision to pass by our field of vision every few minutes with a crazy eye. I may never know. The point is, when facing a potentially dangerous situation, it's better not to go alone. Apparently, Jesus agreed, as He chose to send His disciples out two-by-two.

Most of us probably don't think of a preaching and healing ministry as particularly *dangerous*. But let us be reminded that these men were waging war, not only against sin and sickness, but also against the spiritual forces of Satan. Look again at the description of the man whose demons were exorcised by Jesus in Mark 5:

> When Jesus got out of the boat, a man with an evil spirit came
> from the tombs to meet him. This man lived in the tombs, and
> no one could bind him any more, not even with a chain. For he
> had often been chained hand and foot, but he tore the chains
> apart and broke the irons on his feet. No one was strong
> enough to subdue him. Night and day among the tombs and in
> the hills he would cry out and cut himself with stones (Mark
> 5:2-5).

He broke the irons on his feet? No one was strong enough to subdue him? This is a picture, not merely of a poor lost soul in need of assistance; rather, due to the demonic presence in his body, he had become a wild man, uncontrollable by an entire town of people, even after they had resorted to chaining him up! Think about the potential for harm to these disciples on such a journey. Not only were they likely to be rejected by people (Mark 6:11), but they also ran the risk of physical and spiritual abuse at the hands of demonic forces. If ever there was a time to have a friend by your side, this was it!

Surely, then, there was a sense in which the pairings by Jesus were quite practical. Matthew Henry remarks that such cooperation served to teach these men to "both lend and borrow help."[8] That is, as a pair, they could readily strengthen both the hands and the

---

[8] Henry, M. (1960). *Matthew Henry's Commentary on the Whole Bible in One Volume.* Grand Rapids, MI: Zondervan, p. 1376.

hearts of their partners. Walter Wessel, however, notes that this strategy was more about the Jewish custom of the day. Specifically, "the purpose of their going in pairs was so that the truthfulness of their testimony about Jesus might be established 'on the testimony of two or three witnesses' (Deut. 17:6)."[9] In other words, he is suggesting that Jesus sent these men out by twos so that their preaching would have credibility amongst the Jewish people.

So who is right? Ultimately, I see no reason why we shouldn't understand both men to be correct in their assessment. After all, just as their assignment was threefold (they were to preach repentance, to heal the sick, and to cast out evil spirits), so, too, perhaps, was the benefit of partnering. By going out in pairs, their preaching would be seen as credible, their hands would be strengthened against the spiritual forces of darkness, and their hearts would be encouraged amidst the tremendous burden of the masses suffering from illness and disease. Thus, not only did Jesus grant them authority to carry out this ministry, but He also established the priority of *community* and *fellowship* in His service. These seemingly ill-prepared young men were called upon to do the impossible – but in more than one way, they were assured that they would not be alone. This did not mean, however, that their journey would not still require a tremendous measure of faith.

The Source of Provision

Imagine being sent on a heroic journey of this sort without provision of any kind. Doesn't it seem strange that Jesus sends these guys out on their own for the first time – their first big-boy trip – and then tells them, "Oh, by the way ... don't take anything"? Don't take bread, he tells them, or even a bag to hold your lunch (so you're not tempted to fill it?). Don't take any money whatsoever. You can wear sandals (if you must) ... but don't take an extra shirt. And although Mark's account differs on this final prohibition, both Matthew and Luke report that Jesus told them not to even take along a staff to prop you up if you get tired! Yikes!

I don't like to go anywhere without backup supplies. If I think I might possibly sweat, I'll stow away some deodorant and an extra t-shirt. If I'm going somewhere and there's a chance another person will irritate me into a headache, I take ibuprofen. If I have to speak, I won't go somewhere without cough drops. If I may be eating

---

[9] Gaebelein, p. 667.

foods with which I'm unfamiliar, I always have a few antacids in tow. And food? Don't get me started. I won't even walk the dog without a snack for emergencies. When I read through this list of prohibited supplies, I get nervous and sweaty just thinking about it. But what if I need ... *something*?!

Why do I obsess in this way? Why do some of you? Our tendency, it seems, is to convince ourselves that we are much more secure if we can surround ourselves with items of comfort and means of support. This, of course, is rooted in a very basic fear that when a situation gets unpleasant, we will not be able to maintain control of our environment. What if I get hungry? I better pack some food. What if I get tired? I better take a walking stick. What if I am stranded? Or dirty? Bring money. Take a tunic. The list goes on for each of us, but the underlying assumption is always the same: *if I run into problems, I am going to need to be prepared to resolve them myself.*

Such an approach seems noble, responsible ... perhaps even wise. And yet, Jesus wanted something more from His followers. What He required from them was a genuine faith in the power of God to provide for their needs. By commanding them to eschew supplies of any kind, He was putting them in a position of complete reliance on the Lord. If they grew hungry, they were to trust that God would make a way for them to eat. If they were weary and in need of shelter, they were to humbly receive lodging from the first person who offered it (v. 10). If they needed help walking or climbing the rocky terrain, they were to lean on the partner Jesus Himself had given them. In every way, these men were to live in constant reliance on God alone.

Now, does this mean that none of us ought to make plans, come prepared, or exercise good judgment, *ever* in life? I do not believe this passage prohibits that, universally. And yet, His instruction in this context was clear – perhaps even illustrative: just as you need divine *power* to carry out these tasks, so do you need divine *providence* for your very sustenance on the journey. Put another way, I can't help but wonder if their *physical* dependence was meant to serve as a daily reminder of the depth of their need for God as they healed the sick, preached repentance, and battled demons in the villages. Just as it would be easy to assume that they were responsible for their own physical comfort and provision, they could also be tempted to believe that any success they experienced in ministry was due to their own righteousness and/or power. Jesus wasn't going to let that temptation come into play.

No, they would walk by faith in every aspect of the journey; they would have to trust God for their provision as well as for power. And in the end, we find that this, too, fits the theme of the mission: you are going to do the impossible, but this is not about you. Your ministry will be an extension of mine; I've both modeled and given authority to you to do this. Your journey is not that of a lone ranger: I'm sending you with one another, because you can't do this alone. And just so you're clear on who is behind your success, I don't even want you to think that you provided for your own comfort – that's all God as well. So now, go – I'm sending you!

... And Us Too?

So what about you and me? Are we to understand this as our commissioning too? Have *we* been given authority over evil spirits and the power to bring healing to the diseased? Perhaps C. E. B. Cranfield said it best when he commented, "The particular instructions apply literally only to this brief mission during Jesus' lifetime; but in principle, with the necessary modifications according to climate and other circumstances, they still hold for the continuing ministry of the Church."[10] In other words, it is right to suggest that this was a mission given to these Twelve men at a particular point in history. And yet, our role even as the Church today is to continue Christ's ministry of reconciling the world to God (2 Corinthians 5:19-20).

Prior to His death on the cross, Jesus prayed not only for these apostles of His, but also for you and for me (John 17:20-26). Specifically, He prayed that we would "be brought to complete unity to let the world know that you (the Father) sent me and have loved them even as you have loved me." Likewise, as He spoke His final words to His followers in the first chapter of Acts, He informed them (and presumably, all who would receive His Spirit) that "you will receive power when the Holy Spirit comes on you; and you will be my *witnesses* ..." (Acts 1:8). Thus, while we can reasonably agree that Jesus' instructions in Mark 6 were for those men in particular, we must concede that His expectation for the church today is still that we would be empowered by God (Acts 1) to bear witness to God's love for the world (John 17), and to bring *healing* to those who

---

[10] As quoted by Walter Wessel. See Gaebelein, p. 667.

are apart from God (2 Corinthians 5). That sure sounds similar to me.

Of course, in Paul's letter to the Corinthians (referenced above), such *healing* is understood to be spiritual. This obviously raises the question of whether or not we can still, by the power of the Spirit, bring about physical healing and the exorcism of demons. While a thorough discussion of such ministry today is beyond the scope of this chapter, my short answer is, yes. If I believe that the Enemy is still at work in this world, *and* I believe that the same Spirit who empowered them is alive in me, then it stands to reason that God still works in that way today. I confess that I have not personally taken part in such miraculous acts of healing myself; and yet, if God so chooses to use me for that, I will give Him all the glory. If not, I have no reason to doubt the reports of healing and exorcism administered in our day by followers of Christ all over the world.

That being said, it seems that our tendency is often to seek out (and pontificate on) the *physically miraculous*, while we dismiss the more common way He uses us to bring healing today: through *faithful prayer*. This is why I would suggest that, if we are interested to know how this commission applies to us in our day, the fifth chapter of James paints a fabulous picture:

> *Is any one of you sick? He should call the elders of the church to pray over him and anoint him with oil in the name of the Lord. And the prayer offered in faith will make the sick person well; the Lord will raise him up. If he has sinned, he will be forgiven. Therefore, confess your sins to each other and pray for each other so that you may be healed. The prayer of a righteous man is powerful and effective ... My brothers, if one of you should wander from the truth and someone should bring him back, remember this: whoever turns a sinner from the error of his way will save him from death and cover over a multitude of sins (James 5:13-16, 19-20).*

Here is my point: it would surely be a sensational story if I touched a cancerous patient and that murderous disease completely left his body. The community would be buzzing if a crazy, chain-bursting madman with super-human strength, knelt at my feet as I called on the name of Jesus to set him free. And who knows, maybe one day both of those will happen. But in the meantime, I am surrounded by those who are sin-sick; I am awash in a land of people headed for spiritual death, whom God is desperate to raise up into forgiveness. What am I doing for them? What are you doing for them?

James suggests that whoever turns a sinner from the error of his way will save that person from death and cover a multitude of sins! James says that those of you who have been made righteous (by the blood of Christ) have the power to claim healing for those in need – that your prayers are powerful and effective! He says that the prayer offered in faith will make the sick person well – why? Because *the Lord will raise him up*! While it may be an enticing exercise in theological prowess to debate whether or not we are all empowered and called to preach, heal, and cast out demons today, I would argue that our first step ought to be a faithful ministry with the spiritually sick, whom He has placed all around us already.

So how do we do that? Thankfully, we have been offered a helpful pattern of obedience in commissioning of the original Twelve: first, *we must learn to embrace our role as the extension of the ministry of Christ.* Specifically, we must come to the place where we move from observer to participant in the ministry of reconciliation. Our fear[11] is that we are simply not ready. We fret that we don't know the Scripture well enough, that we will fail; or, in the desperate words of Moses (Exodus 4:13), God simply needs to "send someone else to do it!" Like a terrified, illogical teenager, dangling 170 feet from the ground, we imagine that perhaps we can just stay here forever, never having to pull that cord. But in so doing, we're effectively suspended in the air, failing to bring to fruition the very purpose for which we were called. What I mean is, Jesus didn't call you and save you just so that you could go to Heaven. He set you free so that you could be a *royal priesthood*, leading others into new life. How do we know this is true? We need look no further than His original call to Peter, Andrew, James and John. Remember when He told them, "Follow me, and *I'll show you a bunch of miracles*?" Me neither. What He said was, "I will make you fishers of men." Carrying on the redemptive ministry of Christ was always the plan for them. The same is true for you and me – but we'll never walk in that purpose until we're willing to be sent.

So first, we need to accept our calling to participate. Secondly, we must *willingly join others in this ministry.* For some of us, this element comes as a great relief (as it should!): you do not

---

[11] Or should I say, *excuse*?

have to go at this alone! He is not looking for brave *individuals* to do His bidding; Christ has called the Church – the unified body – to go together, learn together, pray together, and serve together. Some of us need to hear that we are not meant to be in this by ourselves. However, for others of us, this point comes as a tremendous challenge. Because, after all, people can be difficult! Not everyone agrees with *me*, nor do they want to do everything *my* way (the nerve!). Thus, we have convinced ourselves that some jobs are just easier to do alone, and that we're better off in the company of Christ alone, just doing our own thing. But Jesus knew better. As God the Son, He had existed eternally in perfect communion with God the Father and God the Spirit; therefore, as a man in the world, He did almost nothing without taking at least three friends. There's nothing noble about a *loner Christian*; in fact, I'm not even sure that phrase is a logical possibility. It's just not how we were made.

Finally, we cannot follow Christ in this way until we agree to *trust Him completely*. If you've spent a lifetime depending on yourself and your own resources, complete trust likely won't happen by tomorrow. But even now you can take a step in that direction. The disciples did, and God multiplied the ministry of Jesus. Mark tells us that they went out and preached repentance. He adds that they drove out many demons and healed many sick people. Can you imagine the euphoria of seeing God move through you like that? I don't know how ready they felt when they left, but by taking that first step into town, by reaching out their hands for the first time, they exhibited a faith in God that led to victory.

The fact is, you'll probably *never* feel ready to step out into this frightening journey of faith. But that was precisely the point, wasn't it? Jesus said, your authority over the Enemy is coming from me. Your provision is coming through those whom the Father puts in your path. I know you're going to feel neither prepared nor able. But for some of them, maybe that was the only way they'd be sure and give glory to God. Likewise, He wants to bring victory through you. He wants to bring healing and repentance through your ministry in this world. But it doesn't happen until you take that first step, speak that first word, in humble faith.

A Final Word

Before we get to our practical action step, I can't help but notice the placement of this story in the narrative of Mark. I've covered the highlights of all his miracles leading up to chapter six, but look at how this chapter actually begins. After all His amazing works, He enters into His hometown, where "He could not do any miracles there, except lay his hands on a few sick people and heal them" (Mark 6:5). The narrator closes this section by noting that Jesus "was amazed[12] at their lack of faith" (v. 6a). As I pointed out earlier, could this trip be described in any other way than a great disappointment? How do you suppose that experience impacted the hearts of these men who are being called now to take a shot at this same ministry? I mean, had they just come off the exorcism of the crazy man, or the resurrection of the little girl, they might be pumped up for action; but they were commissioned after watching even Jesus seemingly fall short.[13]

I wonder, though, if perhaps this timing was intentional. What I mean is, Jesus *inferred* that not everyone would be receptive to their ministry (Mark 6:11); but maybe they also needed to *see* what that looked like. Is it possible that His message to them was: *just as your provision is outside of your control, so is your success.* Not *every*one will be healed, not *every*one will repent. We even see later in the Gospels that the disciples were not successful in exorcising *every* demon. Neither will you or I be. The pertinent truth is that we cannot control results, nor can we control the faith of others. Jesus doesn't call His followers to a perfect record in ministry. He simply wants us to walk together in faith. He wants us to embrace the urgency of His mission in this world, that all may hear of His love. The adventure begins when you say yes.

As my friends and I dangled there in the stratosphere, I wasn't sure I could release us into the adventure for which we'd prepared ourselves. I don't remember how many times they said "fly" from the ground below, but eventually I pulled the cord. And in truest sense of the word, my friends and I flew together. So can you and yours, in the power of Christ.

---

[12] For whatever it's worth, I've always thought it would be incredible to *amaze* Jesus. Just, you know, not like *that*.
[13] Again, the implication is that it was the *people* whose faith was insufficient, not the power of Jesus.

Practical Action Step

Chances are, you know a person who doesn't know Jesus. That friend (or family member) is in desperate need of help and healing. So find a Christian brother or sister and pray together that God would intervene in that person's life; then get up, go together, and share the Good News with that friend. This is not meant as a license to be invasive, uncaring, or sloppy in your evangelistic venture. Go not as a pair looking to fulfill a duty, but as two people consumed by love for your friend – then share Jesus in the light of that love. As you go, choose to fear neither rejection, disinterest, nor your own insufficiency. Our God is big enough to provide all that each of you needs.

The Other Half

Is it OK for a man to admit that he sort-of likes Kevin Costner movies? In my own circle of friends, Costner is more readily associated with the romantic comedy genre, making such an admission a death knell to one's perceived masculinity. But in my defense, the man has quite a diversified resume when it comes to films. Admittedly, he participated in *Robin Hood: Prince of Thieves* and *Message in a Bottle*, but he also did plenty of manly gun-slinging in *The Untouchables*, *Wyatt Earp*, and the TV mini-series *Hatfields and McCoys*. I therefore stand by my confession.

In one of his more recent films, *The Guardian*, Costner portrays an aging Coast Guard rescue swimmer who has begrudgingly agreed to become a teacher for the younger recruits. Conflict quickly arises in the movie when Costner's character, Ben Randall, butts heads with an arrogant new candidate named Jake Fischer (played by Ashton Kutcher). In one of their earliest formal interactions with one another, Ben explains the first training exercise to the group of newbies: get in the swimming pool and tread water for an hour. Anyone who can't stay above water for that period of time is to be immediately cut from the program.

Right next to Jake in the pool is a muscle-bound recruit who soon struggles to meet the challenge. As the man begins to groan in pain, and as his head starts to dip under the surface, Jake – who is clearly close enough to help out – merely looks on with pity. Within seconds, the recruit finally dips under the water and is removed from both the pool and the program. As Jake swims to the edge of the pool to climb out, Randall questions him about his refusal to help his colleague. He has quickly come to regard Jake as a *me*-first kind of guy, a quality he thoroughly loathes in a person, and this scene in the pool served as exhibit A.

"You saw him struggling," Randall accusingly asks, as he halts the young man's exit with foot on his head, "why didn't you help him?" Somewhat dumbfounded by the very suggestion, Jake sheepishly replies, "I didn't know we were supposed to be working as a team." Clearly disappointed, Randall responds, "*That's the only way we work.*" And in the context of the plot, this scene serves as a critical early indicator of how much Jake still needs to learn throughout the course of the film. That is, his ambivalent attitude towards his fellow recruit in that moment is meant to illustrate his lack of maturity.

But to be honest, what most fascinated me about that entire exchange was my own response as a viewer. Specifically, when Jake just watched this other man stumble and fail (instead of offering some sort of assistance), I experienced the same uncertainty as did the character in the film: was he *supposed* to help him out? Until Ben Randall chastised Jake for his passivity, I was actually wondering the same thing as he was: wasn't this an individual exercise? The thought of bringing someone else along to achieve success wouldn't have really crossed my mind either.

When it comes to rescue swimming for the Coast Guard, I suppose I can give myself a pass for my ignorance. I don't know much about the teamwork expectations involved in their training, so I'll just have to take Kevin Costner's word for it. What troubles me, however, is that I often see much of this same individualistic uncertainty in the life of the church. Here is what I mean: what is our standard response when we see new believers struggling to keep their heads above water, in regards to temptation? What do we do when right next to us is a fellow church-goer whose life is in disarray, and he is on the verge of giving up? Far too often, we seem content to look on in pity, at best offering insincere promises to "be there" or to "pray for you," without ever sensing a real responsibility to reach out and help them continue on to maturity.

Ultimately, many of us have fallen prey to the deception that discipleship is simply about "me and Jesus." That is, any effort we make in this life to follow Christ is usually centered on our own personal journey. We ask questions like, "what does God want *me* to do with *my* life?" and "how can *I* grow closer to Him?" These are both certainly fine questions ... but they're also only half of what it means to be His disciple. Consider again the invitation that Jesus extended to the men on the lake that day: "*Come, follow me, and I will make you fishers of men.*"[1] Without question, the call was made to individuals, that they might walk with the Lord – to learn from Him, even become like Him. But from the very beginning, this discipleship always had an end in sight: that these men would ultimately reproduce themselves in others, just as Jesus had done with them.

What we must begin to understand is that the call to follow Christ is not merely an individual adventure; rather, *to follow Him is to make disciples.* Perhaps this fundamental reality was never more clearly articulated than in the brief address which has become known as the Great Commission:

> *And Jesus came and said to them, "All authority in heaven and on earth has been given to me. Go therefore and make disciples of all nations, baptizing them into[2] the name of the Father and of the Son and of the Holy Spirit, teaching them to observe all that I have commanded you. And behold, I am with you always, to the end of the age." (Matthew 28:18-20, ESV)*

This commissioning of Jesus' followers was not simply offered as a new directive in light of His impending ascension. Instead, it was the very fulfillment of their original call. In other words, discipleship was *always* about making disciples, and Jesus was now bringing that promise to fruition.

I would here submit that the same is true for you and me. We cannot properly conceive of a discipleship (following Jesus) which does not include *making disciples*; it's not an add-on for the highly motivated and specifically gifted Christian; instead, it is the very core of our own faith practice. So as we move forward together in this chapter, we will explore this command by examining two critical and related questions: what does it mean to make a disciple, and how do we go about doing it?

Go and Make Disciples

D. A. Carson points out that the only *actual* command (linguistically) in the Great Commission is to *make disciples.*[3] Specifically, the original author uses the Greek word μαθητεύσατε,

---

[1] Matthew 4:19.

[2] While the ESV first translates this word as "in," the option for "into" is offered as a footnote. As I explain in footnote 10, I am strongly in favor of the translation "into."

[3] Gaebelein, p. 595.

which is written in the imperative mood. Conversely, every other verb (go, baptizing, teaching) in the commission itself is a participle. For any reader unfamiliar with the Greek language, the implication of such a construction is nevertheless quite simple: the force of the command rests with the imperative verb.[4] In this case, then, it must be noted the Great Commission is ultimately a command *to make disciples*; every other verb in the construction serves to support that. To put it another way, the Great Commission is not fulfilled simply by going, teaching, or even baptizing. He was telling His disciples that making other disciples was an absolute must.

If, therefore, this command to make disciples is that significant, then what does it mean? Sadly, I would argue that our failure to properly understand this concept has often led the church into premature celebration. Let me give you an example: as I mentioned in an earlier chapter, for several months now, my congregation has been taking advantage of a tremendous opportunity to lead a time of worship with the residents of a local correctional facility. Every time we have worshipped with them thus far, we've left incredibly encouraged by the generally exuberant response these residents offer up to the Lord.

On a recent trip, as has become our practice, I extended an invitation for the residents to respond to the message they'd just heard on forgiveness and having a fresh start in Jesus Christ. If you want to be made clean, I told them, will you stand up where you are? Out of the 50 or so people in attendance, 35 stood up. We invited them to come and pray with our team, and then we closed in song. It was easily the largest response we'd seen in our time there, and all of us returned to the church van just buzzing with excitement. We came home and shared with our congregation that these 35 residents had responded to the grace of God – praise His name!

As I reflect on that day, none of what I have described (to our church or to you, the reader) is inaccurate. Thirty-five people responded in some way to the Lord. But had we *made 35 disciples* that day? Let's just assume, for argument's sake, that every one of

---

[4] For what it's worth, Carson adds that we must be careful here not to quickly assume that *going* is merely optional (i.e., "as we go"). He points out that "when a participle functions as a circumstantial participle dependent on an imperative, it normally gains some imperatival force." Simply put, because of its connection to *make disciples* in the Greek sentence construction, *go* has a little added thrust (as a command) as well. Gaebelein, p. 595.

those individuals who stood made a sincere confession to the Lord. They had their souls awakened to His grace, and many may have even trusted Him for full forgiveness on that day. But mere moments after they'd made such a decision, we walked out the door, seeing many of them for the last time.[5]

For all we know, some may have fallen by the wayside and been devoured by the enemy. Some may have made a shallow commitment in the moment, only to wither up when trials came. Perhaps others returned that same day to a group of unsupportive fellow-residents, and that spark which earlier burned inside their hearts was quickly snuffed out.[6] By the grace of God, others may today be pointing to that moment as the launching pad of their new life in Christ. The point is, we do not know for sure. And we do not know, because we are not there with them. You see, making disciples is not simply a matter of spreading the seed of the Gospel and inviting people to say the sinner's prayer; making disciples runs deeper, takes longer, and requires more from everyone involved.

Jesus once described it this way: *If anyone would come after me, he must deny himself and take up his cross daily and follow me. For whoever wants to save his life will lose it, but whoever loses his life for me will save it* (Luke 9:23-24). Again, the concept points back to His original invitation to Peter, Andrew, James and John. We've already noted that the "follow me" came with a purpose: that He would make them fishers of men. But we must also consider the weight of the first part of His statement in Luke 9; specifically, that becoming His disciple was not simply a matter of saying a prayer and agreeing to truths. If a person was going to be the disciple of Jesus, it was going to require a fully invested relationship.

Please don't misunderstand my point: leading someone to the place of confession in Christ is both a beautiful and critical element of evangelism. I wholeheartedly contend that in that moment of genuine profession of faith in the name of Jesus, a person is justified and moves from death to life. The problem, however, is that the church is too often satisfied to leave a person there. We rejoice that God has rescued the sinner, but we forget that He has

---

[5] Why for the last time? The nature of this facility is such that residents will not spend more than about six months onsite; they are here finishing up their terms, generally speaking. For our part, we rotate with a group of other churches doing the same thing, and our turn comes only once every 1-2 months.

[6] See the parable of the sower: Matt. 13; Mark 4; Luke 8.

called us to a deeper fellowship. That trip to the altar, that prayer uttered in remorse, was only meant to serve as the *starting point* of full-fledged discipleship. And that discipleship only occurs when a teacher looks to a student and says, "Follow me."

Follow me as I live out my faith in the marketplace. *Follow me* as I model a godly home life. *Follow me* as I serve others, submit my will, and honor God in all things. In the case of Jesus and His Twelve, the pattern was clear: He called them to follow Him (to literally go where He went), He carried out God's redemptive mission as they observed, He empowered them to reproduce that ministry alongside Him, and then He launched them into the teaching role in His absence. Effectively, He reproduced Himself in them, that they might do the same in others.[7] But it didn't happen in a singular moment of decision; He taught them, admonished them, encouraged them and empowered them over the course of three years.

Have you ever invested yourself in the spiritual development of another to that same degree? Your Savior has commanded it – in fact, it's the very reason He called you to follow Him! Again, making disciples is not simply an optional ministry for the specially equipped; making disciples is what it means to follow Jesus. It is the central imperative thrust of the Great Commission. So how do we do it? Jesus indicated that the primary marks of the disciple-making process are baptism and teaching.[8]

Baptize Them Into the Name

When I was in seventh grade, I started a club, which I cleverly named *The Family*. As much as I would like to tell you that it was some sort of smooth spin-off of *The Godfather*, it was actually just *a* family; as in, each person had a role (i.e., father, mother, son, daughter, etc.).[9] It's not like I was the most popular guy in school, so my potential for success in the initiation of a club was tenuous at best. That said, I was nothing if not shrewd, and so I came up with a foolproof strategy. I would be the father, of course, but I would

---

[7] For instance, see John 17:6-20.

[8] Carson is quick to point out that the Greek syntax prevents us from regarding baptizing and teaching as strictly being the *means* of making disciples. Yet, he concedes that these verbs certainly *characterize* it. See Gaebelein, p. 597.

[9] Ok, so in hindsight, it sounds like I didn't so much start up a clever club, as much as I was just *playing house* ... in seventh grade. Self-esteem plummeting ...

select the most popular kids in my class to fill in the other roles. And against all odds, these other kids seemed to go for it.

Sadly, my victory proved to be short-lived. Within about an hour of establishing *The Family*, I came upon a conversation where the girl I'd tabbed to be the mother was describing the club to someone else. As she did so, she listed off the names of those filling the various roles; yet, mysteriously, I heard someone else's name inserted into the position of the father. Curious, I injected myself into the conversation, saying, "No, don't you remember? I'm the father."

"Well, you *were*," she said flatly, "but we decided to kick you out."

Ouch. It's hard to describe the emotional low which accompanies the realization that you're not even cool enough to be a part of the club that you made up. Still, the incident has always served as a poignant reminder of the sense of significance that comes with being part of a family. Graciously, God showed me the full impact of this reality at the age of 8.

Sometime prior to my second birthday, my parents divorced and went their separate ways. This left me – with my sister – in a single parent home with my mother. Although we were able to visit with my biological father from time to time at first, over the course of the next few years, those visits became few and far between. Whereas once we visited his house (and his new family) with some regularity, our time together was soon relegated to trips to local fast food restaurants. Before long, the phone calls ceased, as did any communication whatsoever. While this parental void in my life was all I'd ever really known, there were still some days when I struggled to find an identity because of it.

After I turned six, my mom met a wonderful man named Dave Bash, whom she would marry the following year. He loved us and provided for us; and for the first time, I began to experience a taste of what it was like to have a father who was present in my life. After their wedding, we all lived together as a patchwork family for about half a year, until one day Mom and Dave came in my room and sat me down on the bed. They asked me what I would think about my step-dad legally adopting me. He would become my dad *officially*, and I would be his son. I would take on his last name (as would my sister), and we would become a real family in the fullest sense. That sounded like a pretty great deal to me!

While my memories of the official proceedings in the courthouse that day are fleeting, what I do remember well was the feeling I had afterwards. We went out to a park to celebrate, and I felt like I was walking on air. The sun was shining, the clouds had disappeared, and for the first time in my life, I knew what it was like to have a real dad. This man had loved me, had given me his name, and had promised to take care of me for as long as I needed him. Over the course of the next 25 years or so, my dad invested his life in mine, modeling the kind of Christ-like character that I hope he would say has been reproduced in me. And it all began that day that he decided to give me his name and make me a part of his family.

Undoubtedly, the various traditions of Christianity have all taken a position on the precise significance and meaning of *baptism* in the life of a believer. And while we may not all agree on all the specific nuances of this sacred practice, one reality upon which most of us can likely reach consensus is that, for the early church, baptism marked one's entrance into the family of God. And so without igniting a debate on the specifics of the sacrament itself, I would simply suggest that, at the very least, Jesus' words in the Great Commission indicated that *making disciples would first be characterized by welcoming new believers into the covenant community of Christ.*

The crucial evidence in support of such a claim is, unfortunately, often overlooked. In my own denomination (as in many others), whenever we baptize a believer, we utilize what has become known as the *baptismal formula*: "I baptize you in the name of the Father, and of the Son, and of the Holy Spirit." To be sure, to do so is not theologically problematic. However, when we regard these words *merely* as a formula, I would argue that we miss the point of what Christ said. To illustrate what I mean, let us examine this phrase in two parts.

For starters, we must first consider the word most often translated as "in." In the Greek text, the word originally used was εἰς, which primarily indicates "a movement into," rather than the more static "in."[10] Secondly, it is worth pointing out that "the name" is a singular noun; yet, it is attributed to the three Persons of the Father, Son and Spirit. Thus, it is reasonable to surmise that Jesus here had

---

[10] Will I fight to the death on this point? I will not. It is certainly grammatically acceptable to translate this word as "in;" however, given the context, I find the primary meaning of the word to be a much more appropriate translation.

the Trinity in mind. Put another way, a convert is not simply baptized *in the names of* the Father, Son and Spirit (as a formula); rather, it would be more accurate to say that he is *baptized into the Triune name*. The implication, of course, is that baptism functions as (among other things) *a movement into the communion of the Church, which herself models the unity of the Triune God.*[11]

So what is it that I am here suggesting? Put simply, the call to *make disciples* is first a call to usher new believers into the full fellowship of the family of God. And by this, I am pointing not only to the actual event of baptism; in terms of welcoming a person into the body of Christ, it is more than a dip in the water and a pat on the back. *I am talking about making these believers a part of the family in the same sense that my dad brought me into his.* Surely the moment the judge in the family court banged his gavel was of great legal significance. In that instant, I became a Bash. But if my dad's investment in my life had ended there, I would hardly be able to speak of being a part of a family. Instead, it was his love, devotion, and presence in my life over the next several years that made me a part of his household. The same is true in the life of the Church.

This is perhaps the most glaring evidence that what our congregation does in the correctional facility cannot be described as *making disciples.* As wonderful and vital as our ministry there is, we cannot make disciples without investing in intentional and enduring relationships with others. Dietrich Bonhoeffer has suggested that even "the physical presence of other Christians is a source of incomparable joy and strength to the believer."[12] Thus, making disciples must surely include such a commitment to community, as is inherent in the sacrament of baptism; and yet, Jesus did not leave it at baptism alone.

Teaching Them to Obey

As the example of my own adoption perhaps infers, the second crucial characterization of one who is making disciples is that she is *teaching others to obey all that Christ has commanded.* As anyone who has raised children could likely attest, this is no easy task. About a year ago, my wife and I decided that it was time our

---

[11] Jesus' prayer found in John 17:20-26 offers further evidence that this is precisely His plan for the Church: to share in and reflect the unity which He shares with the Father.

[12] Bonhoeffer, D. (1954). *Life Together: The Classic Exploration of Faith in Community.* San Francisco, CA: HarperCollins, p. 19.

children learn a little something about money management. Simultaneously, we felt they were of the age where they could meaningfully contribute to household chores; so, we instituted the Bash Family Chore Chart. First, each chore listed on the chart (such as folding laundry, washing dishes, vacuuming, etc.) was assigned a monetary value, based on both the difficulty and time commitment of the task. Then, whenever a child would do the chore, we would mark down the day it happened, then settle up with cash at the end of the week.[13]

What we soon discovered was that each child had a collection of chores they preferred to do, and on my daughter's list was folding and putting away laundry. This was alright in my book, as that had primarily been one of my duties before the institution of the chore chart.[14] So for weeks, we sent her upstairs with the laundry basket, which she would return to us empty after several minutes. We held up our end of the deal and paid her accordingly at the end of each week, never asking any questions about her laundry strategy. To be honest, I was pretty satisfied simply that someone else was doing it.

This went on for a while, until one day when her mother went into her room to find a shirt, only to discover that all her dresser drawers seemed to be stuck. As my wife investigated further, she soon recognized the source of the problem: for weeks, my daughter had been wadding shirts and pants into what barely resembled a fold, then stuffing them in the [sometimes] appropriate drawers. With little regard for the capacity of said drawers, our little girl had just continued to stuff until the drawers would no longer open properly. As we questioned her methods, we soon came to an embarrassing conclusion: although we had clearly communicated to our daughter *what* we wanted her to do, we had failed to teach her *how to do it*.[15]

Likewise, a pastor friend commented to me the other day that our standard operating procedure within the church is often to merely "Teach them ... everything I have commanded you," rather

---

[13] FYI, the cash is then divided four ways: tithe, savings, money for gifts, and spending money. This idea did not originate with me. See Friedeman's *Discipleship in the Home*.

[14] Thus, the hidden treasure of the chore chart – less work for me! Just kidding, kind of.

[15] My wife might argue that my daughter's laundry methods were, in point of fact, learned directly from me, but that's neither here nor there.

than teaching them TO OBEY the commands of Jesus. His distinction here is surely astute! His point, of course, is that we have convinced ourselves that our job is done when we simply tell people *what* Jesus said; but as the text clearly indicates, Jesus instructed us, as we make disciples, to go further and teach them *how to obey*, as well.

When it comes to children, this concept is easy enough. In the context of a hands-on job in ministry, a woman in our congregation has helpfully reduced child-training down to a simple three-stage procedure: 1) I'll do and explain the job, while you watch, 2) you instruct me how to do the job, and 3) you do the job, while I watch. By utilizing that strategy, she has successfully taught a number of children how to perform various tasks around the church. And perhaps in the course of making disciples, you may find a place for a formal procedure like this. But more often than not, learning to obey the teaching of Christ happens in the *informality* of life. Likely, you will be called upon to teach others to obey in the context of day-to-day relationship – so how can we best teach others to obey?

First, we must be willing to teach disciples just what it is that Jesus taught. At first glance, this perhaps seems as if it goes without saying. We can't teach them to obey unless we ... *teach* them. Genius! Still, ask yourself whether or not you've been intentionally teaching others about the commands of Jesus. I would suggest that such a commitment requires two things that many of us lack: a proficient knowledge of the Scripture and the courage to hold *Christians* accountable to it.

It is often startling to me how many long-time church-goers will randomly insert worldly "wisdom" (or even tenets of other religions) into a theological discussion, as though they are quoting Scripture. The last time I heard a believer assert, "Well, I think God just wants me to be happy," I nearly choked on my own tongue trying to ask about the source of that particular nugget.[16] Listen, I'm not suggesting that every believer needs a Ph.D. in biblical interpretation – but if we're going to make disciples, it would probably help that we are continuing on to spiritual maturity ourselves, wouldn't it? If I have been following Christ for any amount of time, I ought to at least have a pretty good sense of what He taught, how He lived, and what He required of His disciples.

---

[16] I'm not trying to be unnecessarily harsh. I'm sure God loves it when we're happy ... but to suggest that my temporal happiness is His singular priority is to fail to understand the whole of Scripture.

Otherwise, any attempt to teach another about all Christ has commanded will merely result in the reproduction of *your own opinions* – not the character of our Lord.

If, then, we are to teach the word, we must know it as well as possible. And as we do, we must, secondly, *refuse to run from it.* Let's be honest: we have come to the place in our society where referring to sin for what it is can widely be regarded as "hate speech." Due not only to cultural pressure from the outside, but oftentimes pressure from those inside our congregations as well, it is easy to tiptoe around those activities which Scripture deems wicked. And trust me – if it is hard enough to call out sin from the relative security of a pulpit, I can surely appreciate the difficulty involved in holding our Christian brothers and sisters accountable on a personal level.

But how much do you really love them? What I mean is, sometimes our fellow believers know that they're walking far from the Lord, but no one has had the courage to hold them accountable in a restorative, loving manner. Teaching must not be limited to the theoretical, or to the sins we consider to be "major." Teaching means knowing and loving a fellow disciple well enough that you can gently challenge obvious sin in their lives.

So first, teaching them to obey must include informed, courageous teaching. But if they're going to truly learn to submit to Jesus, we must also be willing to *model* obedience as well, that they may see the fruit of a life well-lived. For me, this reality has really hit home in recent years. My son is now nearly ten years old, and it is remarkable to see the subtle ways in which he is transitioning from a boy to a young man. It is apparent in the way that he converses with us, the way he reasons, and the way he cares for others. He is a wonderful boy, and as his father, it is a joy to watch him grow.

But the older he gets, the more I see in him some of the same tendencies that I exhibit at home. By the grace of God, I would like to think that many of those tendencies are holy. If I'm honest, I would have to confess that some of them are not. I watch him struggle, at times, to be patient with his sister. I watch him, every once in a while, speak to his mom out of frustration. And every time I do, I am usually able to remember recently seeing myself do the very same thing. You see, largely, our children are going to treat others just like their parents do. My son is probably going to treat his mother and his wife just like he sees me do it. My daughter is going to expect to be treated in a relationship just like she sees me respond to her mom. If you're giving, humble and kind, they'll likely model that. But if you're cold, vindictive and manipulating, you'll likely see that surface in their personalities too.

Ultimately, I find that the same is true when we talk about *spiritual* parents and children. What kind of life are you modeling for those you are discipling, whether it's in your own home or in the context of the church? If new Christians see that you are a servant, never seeking recognition or demanding your own way, they'll learn that what Jesus taught about servanthood really can be lived out. But if they hear you talking about the importance of love and integrity, then watch you exhibit neither, they'll learn to compartmentalize their Christianity, just like you have.

Again, like children, young Christians are likely to develop the same patterns as their spiritual mentors. So if you're going to teach them to obey all that Christ has commanded, then be sure that your own body is being offered as a living sacrifice, holy and pleasing to God (Romans 12:1). Be sure that your teaching and the pattern of your life are consistent in faithfulness to God, so that one day, these fresh disciples into whom you've poured yourself, can go and likewise reproduce Christ in others.

To live for any other purpose is to deny the call of Christ. "Come follow me," He said, "and I will make you fishers of men." And thus we see that genuine discipleship must include both: as He continually leads me, shapes me and grows me, I am likewise offering the fullness of His life to others. The truth is, *we are not all on our own out there.* We were created to reflect the image of the Triune God, and we were called to follow Jesus, that we might lead others to Him. In the end, discipleship can be nothing less.

Practical Action Step

Although this is likely true for *many* of the practical action steps, this one in particular necessitates this reminder up front: *you will not have completed the action of making disciples in one day.* As it has hopefully been made clear above, discipling others takes time. It involves a significant investment in the life of another, and it cannot be accomplished by simply taking one step. That said, we certainly can commit today to taking that first step. So where do we begin?

If you are a new believer, I would suggest that your first step ought to be to invite a disciple-maker to speak into your life. While you likely can lead others to a deeper knowledge of Christ, even at your current stage, you will be far more successful if you have seen it effectively modeled in your own life. So this week, prayerfully consider whom God might use to teach and model life in the family of God for you. Then, when you have prayed, go ask him or her[17] to walk with you as you seek to reach maturity in the Lord. Plan a time to meet together so that you can both be specific about what this relationship would look like. Don't just leave the request in vague terms, because discipleship is most assuredly an *intentional* endeavor.

If you are one who has been discipled before, and you have good reason to believe that you are in a position to mentor others in the faith,[18] ask the Lord this very moment to lead you to a person young in the faith, whom you could come alongside in this capacity. If it helps, give thought ahead of time to what this arrangement might involve. And as He places someone on your heart – and I believe He will if we ask – extend an invitation of discipleship.

---

[17] Men ask men, women ask women ... do I need to say this? We must always avoid even the hint of impropriety.
[18] I would strongly suggest looking outside your own self-assessment to answer this question. Ask a trusted, mature Christian (who knows you) to speak honestly to you about your preparedness to disciple others.

Coming in Last

As we raced around the track for our final lap, my confidence was soaring. He and I had gone head to head more times than I could count, and, not to toot my own horn, but my record against him was pretty solid. Even though he'd been on a hot streak of late, beating me rather consistently, I was certain I was still the better driver. These last few weeks have just been a fluke, I told myself. Now, as I found myself in the lead, racing toward the finish line, it seemed like order had been restored to the universe. But just as I was preparing to float across the line, gearing up for some spirited trash talk, my car was jarred from behind. Before I could figure out what in the world had happened, I found myself staring at his taillights as I reached the finish. He had beaten me again.

"This is ridiculous," I muttered to myself, as I slammed the steering wheel. Mercifully, he didn't say much after his victory. But to be honest, that may have made it worse. He wasn't even that excited to beat me anymore; he just expected it. As my confidence now plummeted, I went and sought solace from my wife. "I don't think I'm going to race him anymore," I told her.

"You're not going to play a video game[1] with your son? Ever again?"

"Probably not."

"Why?"

"Because I can't beat him!" Somehow, she thought this was funny.[2] "He's nine years old!" I continued. "I'm supposed to have at least ... six more years before he can beat me at anything!"

---

[1] *MarioKart* on the Nintendo Wii, in case you're interested. I created a crazy-eyed character named Boss Hog, just to intimidate him when we race each other.

[2] Funny in a "wow-my-husband-is-pathetic" sort of way.

"You know these games are supposed to be fun, right?" she asked.

"They *are* fun. When I win, like I'm supposed to. Maybe I can get him to play me in a real game of basketball." I was getting desperate. And it was at this point that I began to realize I have a problem: *I need to win.* Trust me when I tell you that I usually hide it pretty well. Being a pastor, I know that if I lose, I can't tip over board games at friends' houses, or throw fits on the basketball court at church camp. But deep inside, if I'm honest with myself, I don't generally play games for fun. I play because it's an opportunity to win; and in case I didn't mention it before, I *love* to win. The first time my flag football team won the intramural championship at our college, I stood on the field and cried as the clock ran down to zero. To this day, I still have the t-shirt from when my friends and I won the junior high church-league basketball tournament ... 20 years ago.

As I have reflected over the years on why, despite my best efforts, my competitive nature comes surging forth in everything – from playing *Candyland* with my kids, to watching my favorite NBA team chase the title – I have come to the conclusion that I often attach my own self-worth to winning. That is to say, if I win, it means I'm important. I *matter*, because I was the best at a given task (even if that task was simply rooting for the right pro basketball team). And that is precisely the draw of competition, broadly speaking. Ultimately, games afford us the opportunity to answer that age-old question amongst human beings all over the world: *which one of us is the greatest?*

Isn't it striking how often we see the disciples of Christ wrestling with this very same issue? It came up on the road as they traveled together (Mark 9:34), some privately sought advancement in His kingdom (Mark 10:37), and the gospel-writer Luke tells us that such a dispute arose even at the Last Supper (Luke 22:24). Yet, as Richard Foster has astutely noted, "whenever there is trouble over who is the greatest, there is trouble over who is the least. That is the crux of the matter for us, isn't it? Most of us know we will never be the greatest; just don't let us be the least."[3]

This was surely what was at stake when Jesus and the Twelve were gathered for their final hours together before the cross. As the evening meal was being served, a sobering reality was quickly descending on them all: *their feet stunk.* Unfortunately, no one had

---

[3] Foster, R. (1978). *Celebration of Discipline: The Path to Spiritual Growth.* San Francisco, CA: HarperCollins, p. 126.

bothered to see to it that a proper servant was available to wash their feet, prior to eating. As you may already be aware, such a cleansing was the custom of the day in Palestine. Due in large part to the dusty roads of the region, coupled with the open sandals worn by nearly everyone, the host[4] normally provided water, a towel, and often a slave, to clean the dirt from the feet of his guests.[5] Yet, in the absence of such a foot-washer, one of them would need to step up; because, of course, the job still needed to be done.

Or perhaps we should say that one of them needed to step *down*. Foot-washing was the job of a slave, not of a disciple. In fact, John the Baptist referenced this type of service to establish "his standard of the lowest and meanest kind of service that could be required of any man (John 1:27)."[6] And therein was the problem: for any one of these apostles to volunteer to wash the feet of the others would be tantamount to conceding his own inferiority within the group.[7] To stoop down and kneel at the feet of another would be an outright admission that, not only is he *not* the greatest among them, but that he is clearly the *least*. And as we have seen, none of the Twelve were prepared to make such a concession.

So, were they openly arguing in that moment about who would do it? Were they silently avoiding eye contact with one another, stubbornly recalling their dispute from moments earlier (Luke 22:24)? It's hard to say for sure. We only know what happened next:

> It was just before the Passover Feast. Jesus knew that the time had come for him to leave this world and go to the Father. Having loved his own who were in the world, he now showed them the full extent of his love. The evening meal was being served, and the devil had already prompted Judas Iscariot, son of Simon, to betray Jesus. Jesus knew that the Father had put all things under his power, and that he had come from God and was returning to God; so he got up from the meal, took off his outer clothing, and wrapped a towel around his waist. After that, he poured water into a basin and began to wash his disciples' feet, drying them with the towel that was wrapped

---

[4] In this case, Peter and John by default, per Luke 22:8.
[5] Carter, p. 437.
[6] Gaebelein, F. (1984). *The Expositor's Bible Commentary, Vol. 9*. Grand Rapids, MI: Zondervan, p. 136.
[7] Ibid.

around him. He came to Simon Peter, who said to him, "Lord, are you going to wash my feet?" Jesus replied, "You do not realize now what I am doing, but later you will understand." "No," said Peter, "you shall never wash my feet." Jesus answered, "Unless I wash you, you have no part with me." "Then, Lord," Simon Peter replied, "not just my feet but my hands and my head as well!" Jesus answered, "A person who has had a bath needs only to wash his feet; his whole body is clean. And you are clean, though not every one of you." For he knew who was going to betray him, and that was why he said not everyone was clean. When he had finished washing their feet, he put on his clothes and returned to his place. "Do you understand what I have done for you?" he asked them. "You call me 'Teacher' and 'Lord,' and rightly so, for that is what I am. Now that I, your Lord and Teacher, have washed your feet, you also should wash one another's feet. I have set you an example that you should do as I have done for you. I tell you the truth, no servant is greater than his master, nor is a messenger greater than the one who sent him. Now that you know these things, you will be blessed if you do them." (John 13:1-17)

In that moment, says Foster, "Jesus took a towel and a basin and redefined greatness."[8] Consequently, He then called his disciples to that same sort of greatness. And if you and I are to come after Jesus, we, too, must be great – only, not in the way we normally define it. To be specific, *following Jesus means that we embrace the life of servitude.* If we would aspire to be first, we must choose to be last. If we long to be great, we must choose to become the servant of all.[9] So what does this kind of life look like? We will get there shortly. But first, it may be helpful to examine what servanthood *isn't*, as well as what servanthood may *cost*.

Servanthood Is Not ...

Despite the fact that I've not been interested in professional wrestling since I was a child,[10] I have become familiar with one of its

---

[8] Foster, p. 126.

[9] See Mark 10:43, 44.

[10] I nearly made this the world's longest footnote, but I ultimately decided to show [some] restraint. For, while I do not understand the fascination that *grown men* have with pro wrestling (um ... no offense, if you're reading

biggest current stars. Dwayne Johnson, aka "The Rock," has vaulted past his wrestling peers (in terms of national recognition), due to his crossover into the realm of action films. But in his role as a professional wrestler, he became famous for his ability to put people in their place, with the help of a simple phrase. Always to a chorus of cheers from his rabid fan base, he would angrily look another man in the eye, point his finger at him, and say, "Know your role and shut your mouth!" In a way, it was The Rock's means of establishing a pecking order. Effectively, he was communicating to another man, you are worth less than me, so you don't get to talk.

In the world of professional wrestling, I imagine that this is precisely the way to go. If you want a man to bend to your will, find a way to reduce his self-worth. Unfortunately, some of us have adopted a similar mantra in the pursuit of a servant's heart. *I believe that the first and greatest myth when it comes to servitude is that becoming a servant to others requires a solid dose of self-loathing.* Or put another way, some of us have convinced ourselves that we ought to serve others because we are little more than insignificant worms. Other people *really are* more valuable than we are, we tell ourselves, and so we probably ought to just know our role and shut our mouths. Oddly, though, this does not seem to me to be the model which Jesus gave His followers.

Look again at how the apostle John describes the lead-in to Jesus' startling act of humility: *Jesus knew that the Father had put all things under his power and that he had come from God and was returning to God (v. 3).* So just before kneeling down to perform the most demeaning act of service which existed in that day, Jesus was acutely aware of three realities: first, He knew that everything was under His authority. ALL things. There in that room, Jesus recognized that the Father had given Him full power over everything that was. Secondly, He was cognizant of the fact that He had come from God. To put it in Pauline terms, He perhaps recalled His voluntary surrender of the glory He shared with the Father, when He made Himself nothing, being made in human likeness (Phil. 2:6-8). Third, He was aware in that moment, that very soon He would once

---

this book), when I was a kid, I was ALL IN. But back in the 80s, we didn't need foul language, middle fingers or rampant vulgarity to enjoy the show. Just give us a Giant (Andre), a Hulk (Hogan), a proud American (Hacksaw Jim Duggan), an Animal who ate foam from the turnbuckle (Steele), and a villainous Arab caricature, whose image was fueled by our national fear (The Iron Sheik). That and a man called "Superfly." I could keep going.

again be exalted. He knew He was preparing to return to the Father, and would soon shed the restraints of His humanity.

It is interesting, isn't it, that just before Jesus washes the feet of his friends, we are reminded of *His own awareness* of His place in the universe? I would submit that the example of service Jesus calls His followers to emulate is not one that begins with low self-esteem. Quite the contrary; I would maintain that the servitude He models begins with the fullest sense of one's own value. Consider but a sampling of what God's word has to say about you:

> *"So God created man in his own image, in the image of God he created him; male and female he created them ... God saw all that he had made, and it was very good." (Gen. 1:27, 31)*

> *"You made [mankind] a little lower than the heavenly beings and crowned him with glory and honor." (Ps. 8:5)*

> *"Look at the birds of the air; they do not sow or reap or store away in barns, and yet your heavenly Father feeds them. Are you not much more valuable than they?" (Matt. 6:26)*

Think about it: those called to embrace servanthood are the followers of Christ. As such, we have the honor of being God's holy temple; He has literally chosen to *dwell in us* as we walk in His light. If ever there were a valuable group of people, would it not be those in whom the Holy Spirit lives? My point is not to inflate our egos, leading us to a sinful arrogance – our value is *completely* a result of *His* creative power, *His* redemptive grace, and *His* abiding presence. The point is simply that we need not demean that value as a prerequisite to service. We are called to serve others, not under the illusion of worthlessness, but with full knowledge of who we are in Christ Jesus.

It is only then that we can, as Paul instructed,[11] take on the same attitude as Christ Jesus. In full knowledge of who we are, we are to yet consider others better than ourselves. With complete awareness of the value God has given us, we are to look not only to our own interests, but to the interests of others. It is only then that our attitude can be the same as His, when He chose not to cling to equality with the Father, even though He was Himself God in very

---

[11] Philippians 2:1-11.

nature. Servanthood is not about loathing myself. It is about knowing myself completely, just as Jesus did, and choosing to set that aside anyway. It is about choosing to love others to the fullest extent, *just as* He modeled for us, with the expectation that in so doing, I will come to a deeper knowledge of Him.

So first, the life of servitude is NOT about self-loathing; it's about knowing myself and knowing Christ. But this is not the only misunderstanding we've adopted when it comes to service. *The second critical myth which we must here dispel is that Christlike servanthood is simply a matter of performing acts.* In my earlier days in ministry, I took a group of students to a local soup kitchen. *Once.* Don't get me wrong, it was a solid experience. There is something incredibly humbling (and rewarding) about preparing and serving food to people who literally would not be eating were it not for our service. And not only did we serve them food, but we sat with the people, talked with them, prayed for them. It was a wonderfully stretching evening for me and for our students.

And at the end of the night, we went back home and felt really good about all we'd done for the needy. Maybe we'd try that again in a few months. As I reflected on our work that night, exultant in my own "humility," three of my students likely went home with different thoughts. Upon arrival at their house, they encountered a familiar scene: their mom in the bathroom carefully bathing her own mother. For several years now, Kathy had been caring not only for her own husband and four kids – three of whom were in my ministry at the time – but also for her handicapped mother. Confined to a wheelchair and lacking the use of both legs, Kathy's aged mom needed help doing just about everything. And so, day after day, in the anonymity and silence of a house out in the country, Kathy carefully assisted, bathed, and cared for her mother.

The only reason I even knew about Kathy's faithful service to her mom was because I asked Kathy about her one day in passing. She neither bragged nor complained about all she'd been doing during those years – she simply answered my questions, without a hint of desire for recognition. Her children had never told me about it, likely because such constant and loving service wasn't *remarkable* to them: that was just who their mom was. Regardless of the messes made, regardless of the time spent, and without concern for the monotony of the work, Kathy continued to love in this way until the day her mother went home to be with the Lord.

And ever since that time, I've begun to understand my foray into the soup kitchen in a new light: what I did that night was an *act of service*; the way Kathy spent her life was *true servanthood*. So what's the difference? Though it is perhaps difficult to distinguish from the outside, the primary difference is internal; specifically, it is found in how we approach the service. It has been said that most Christians don't mind serving others; we just don't want to be treated like a servant. How true! Consider some of the thoughts we often let dictate our actions: *I am more than willing to do a tremendous act of service, as long as everyone applauds my humility. I am happy to take a job behind the scenes at church ... until someone treats me like what I do isn't important. I will give of my time, so long as the recipient is thankful. I will gladly serve, as long as no one* actually *regards me as his servant.* Whether we would admit to such thoughts or not, these are the attitudes of those who are only willing to perform acts of service.

I wonder if this type of thinking was at play in the mind of Peter when he reacted to the sight of the Master kneeling at his own feet. "You shall *never* wash my feet," Peter told him. There was no way he was going to let Jesus stoop so low. "It sounds like a statement of humility; in reality it was an act of veiled pride. Jesus' service was an affront to Peter's concept of authority. If Peter had been the master, he would not have washed feet!"[12] Peter was surely not opposed to hard work. After all, it was his idea to stay up on the mountain and build three shelters for Jesus, Moses and Elijah! Peter had no problem with service, per se; he just didn't like the idea of being seen as a servant. And yet, Jesus responded, "Unless I wash you, you have no part with me" (John 13:8). Without question, Jesus was teaching His followers more than one lesson here;[13] but certainly among them was the inference that if Peter didn't change his understanding about the nature of service, He would never truly know Jesus. Peter's heart, thus far, was only willing to perform acts of service.

Conversely, true servanthood "rests contented in hiddenness. It does not fear the lights and blare of attention, but it does not seek them either ... [it] is free of the need to calculate results. It delights only in the service ... True service comes from a relationship with the

---

[12] Foster, p. 136.
[13] For a fuller treatment on the multiple teaching points of the foot-washing, see Church, L. [Ed.]. (1961). *Matthew Henry's Commentary on the Whole Bible.* Grand Rapids, MI: Zondervan, pp. 1582-1585.

divine Other deep inside."[14] This, of course, is what Jesus modeled for His followers on that night. As we discovered earlier, the generation of His humble act was ultimately His relationship with the Father: He knew what the Father had given Him (authority). He knew the One from whom He came (the Father), and He was certain of Him to whom He would once again return (the Father). It was His relationship with God the Father that prompted His true service, and the same is true of me and you.

Another way to think of it is that *God is love*, and thus, true service is generated by true love. Again, this is what John tells us about Jesus: "Having loved his own who were in the world, he now showed them the full extent of his love" (John 13:1). His service was not simply a duty He performed because He loved the Father; rather, His service was the culmination of the love He had for these men. The same love that exists in the Father abided richly in Jesus; and this is the same love He longs to reproduce in each of us. In the end, He wants more than for His followers to simply perform humble acts of service. He wants us, like Him, to be so filled with the love of God for other people that we willingly set aside our own claims and gladly render even the most demeaning service to others – not for pride or for glory, but simply for the knowledge of Christ Himself. But as you are likely aware by now, knowing and walking with Jesus does not come without a cost.

The Cost of Service

Perhaps it goes without saying that to become a true servant will cost you something. Service itself is a hefty price to pay for some of us! But we do have a tendency, it seems, to convince ourselves that we will always find inherent joy in doing good unto others. And for a while, this is often the case – even when we do not receive recognition or gratitude, we find that there is some measure of joy in what feels like suffering.

Another time in my days as a youth minister, I took a group of students overseas for a short-term mission trip. Early in the week, three very well-meaning young ladies offered to do the dishes for the whole team (over 20 of us) for the whole week. I indicated that my plan was to have everyone contribute to that chore, but the girls were adamant: they wanted to wash dishes as their service to the group. Impressed with their willing hearts (and naïve to the

---

[14] Foster, pp. 128-129.

potential pitfalls), I assented. And without question, for a few days, they cleaned up after their peers gladly. But by mid-week, I was noticing weariness on their faces. A couple more days in, and there was clear frustration. When I asked them what the problem was, I pretty much already knew: "No one is helping us do dishes!" Predictably, no one had bothered to thank them for their service, and consequently, the joy of doing the work quickly faded.

Obviously, then, most of us recognize up front that we can easily become weary of performing monotonous, hidden, and thankless service. Yet, when I speak of the potential *cost*, I have in mind a much heavier price than our own frustration and potential for burnout. For when we move from picking and choosing our acts of service to fully embracing the life of servanthood, we truly become the slave to *all*. And from time to time, that *all* will likely include that certain someone to whom we'd rather not submit.

Consider again that night before the Passover in the Upper Room. As Jesus stripped himself down to the garb of a servant, as he knelt before each of these flawed young men to perform His culture's most degrading service, His heart was overflowing with love. He came to John, the young man who would care for the Lord's own mother in His absence. He looked up at James, who had been with Him in the room when He brought that little girl back from death. He came to the place of Matthew, whose very life was an absolute triumph of the grace of God. He moved on to Peter – loud, brash, impetuous Peter – whom Jesus knew would one day provide a level of leadership for the Church, which Peter himself didn't realize was possible.

And then He took His bowl and moved over again. The dirty feet before Him now belonged to a man who perhaps couldn't look Jesus in the eye. These feet belonged to a man who had spread the Gospel, healed the sick, and exorcised demons in the name of Christ. He was a man who'd seen Jesus perform miracles, who had slept out under the stars with Him, who had laughed and eaten and prayed and learned, and had fully participated in the ministry of Jesus. He was a man whom the Savior loved to the fullest extent. And yet, he was the man who very soon would betray Jesus into the hands of His accusers. He was a man whom the devil had already influenced unto wickedness (v. 2), that Jesus might be led to His death. And as He knelt before *this* man, He gently and carefully washed his feet.

Let that sink in for a moment: *Jesus washed the feet of Judas.* He offered cleansing and the right to have a place with Him in the kingdom ... but His offer would eventually be rejected, thrown back in His face with, of all things, a kiss. Jesus said, all you need to be clean is to have your feet washed; but not all of you *are* clean. His service, then, was *offered* to all, but not all would choose to take hold of its full benefit. Despite the fact that He knew what was in the heart of Judas, and despite the fact that He knew His spiritual service[15] would be rejected, He knelt before Judas anyway and became His servant.

The likelihood is that, as you follow Jesus into a heart and life of true servanthood, you will soon find yourself in the presence of an enemy of your own. And it will be in that moment, when you are faced with the choice to either move on down the line or to kneel and serve, that your motivations will be laid bare. Will you offer your service to someone who has (or continues to) hurt you? Will you submit yourself when you are sure that the result will be painful for you? The point is not that you should go find the most undeserving, ungrateful person you can imagine, then do something kind; for that will only lead to pride. Instead, as Foster points out, true service doesn't even concern itself with another's gratitude. It doesn't worry about cost or results: "It can serve enemies as freely as friends."[16]

How could we ever get there? For many of us, we quickly recognize that we have a long way to go when it comes to serving our enemies. And certainly, it is helpful to be reminded, as were the slaves at Colosse, that even when we serve other people, "it is the Lord Christ [we] are serving."[17] But even such a powerful (and true) admonition does not negate the reality that service will indeed be costly. The hope we have, however, is that as we are being transformed by the Spirit, we will come to the place where we find joy even in this.

Service in Action

What has hopefully become clear by now is that Christlike servanthood is about more than simply *what we do* – it is, at its core, a matter of the heart. It is about reorienting our attitudes to the point where we choose to live in willing submission to others, that we might know Christ and love as He loves. With that said, it is my contention that to speak of a transformed heart with no practical

---

[15] Here I am referring not just to the literal foot-washing, but to the spiritual cleansing to which Jesus is pointing in verse 10.
[16] Foster, p. 129.
[17] Colossians 3:24.

evidence is merely to deceive ourselves. Put another way, *true servanthood has to look like something.* So what does it look like in the day-to-day? When we talk about service, our thoughts immediately go to cleaning toilets, serving at a soup kitchen, or various other similar tasks. And to be sure, these are fine ways to serve. In fact, some of us may have opportunity to do just that.

However, if we are to embrace a life of Christian servitude, it may be helpful to add a few more categories to our current way of thinking, that we might learn to serve others even when all the toilets are clean. Richard Foster, in his work entitled *Celebration of Discipline*, offers several avenues of service "in the marketplace."[18] Stretching us further in our understanding of how we can serve practically, he quite insightfully explores many of the ways which we can be of service to one another daily. I have found them to be so helpful that I want to share a handful of them with you:

The service of guarding the reputation of others. What do you suppose the atmosphere would be like in your workplace if everyone guarded the reputations of their colleagues as fiercely as they protected their own? How might such a commitment transform the environment in your church? How easily we find ourselves sharing an unflattering story about another believer, giving ourselves a pass for our gossip simply because we believe the story to be true. And yet, with the carelessness of our words (or even our willingness to hear the gossip of others), we can do irreparable damage to a brother or sister's reputation. Our service must be rendered not only to the physical bodies of our fellow man, but to every aspect of his personhood.

The service of listening. I must admit – this one nearly killed me when I read it, as I do not find it particularly easy to be a good listener. I am a list-maker by nature. I have spent the last few years of my life learning to navigate the demands involved in my roles as a husband, father, pastor and firefighter, all while working towards a degree. As a result, I have learned to be incredibly efficient with my time. I make a list for each day, then I check the items off one-by-one until I lay down to sleep. And for a task-oriented, time-conscious person like myself, nothing interrupts my busy day quite like the unexpected visitor (or phone call). And yet, as Dietrich Bonhoeffer

---

[18] I am deeply indebted to Foster's tremendous work (as well as to Dietrich Bonhoeffer, who himself clearly inspired Foster), which has obviously heavily influenced this chapter. For a full treatment of these summarized types of service, see Foster, pp. 134-140.

once said, "anyone who thinks that his time is too valuable to spend keeping quiet will eventually have no time for God and his brother, but only for himself and for his own follies."[19] Thus, we are reminded that listening not only offers a service we owe to our brothers and sisters in Christ, but also opens the door for God to speak to us.

The service of sharing the word of life. Do we really believe that God can use us to speak life into another? Think about how many times you've seen a loved one going down a path which leads her far from Christ. Is it your pattern to offer the loving admonition of a friend and fellow servant of God? Or do you bite your tongue, because you don't want to sound judgmental? We fear so many potential repercussions of speaking the truth to others – why do we not more greatly fear the eternal damage of sin in the lives of our fellow man? When we speak the truth and hope of the Gospel, we ought to do so in full humility, grace and love. But we must not shy away from this life-giving service to others.

The service of small things. Not every act of service needs to be worthy of a front page write-up. Sometimes a friend needs to hitch a ride to the store. Sometimes a neighbor needs help moving furniture. Sometimes your spouse needs help unloading the groceries. And inevitably, these small requests for help come at the worst possible times. And yet, as Bonhoeffer notes, "one who worries about the loss of time that such petty, outward acts of helpfulness entail is usually taking the importance of his own career to solemnly."[20] Every now and then, we need to allow ourselves to be interrupted. Every now and again, we need to be willing to lose.

As soon as I finish writing this section, my son wants me to pick up my steering wheel and race him once more. I'll probably get beat.[21] But I'm excited to do it anyway, as I imagine it will be a lot of fun, whether I win or not. Because as I have come to discover, greatness as a dad does not come as a result of being first; greatness comes from simply spending time with my son. He just wants his dad next to him, laughing and playing. And when I lay down my need to win, my selfish grip on my time, and my ridiculous desire for fleeting glory, I find that we both win.

---

[19] Bonhoeffer, D. (1954). *Life Together: The Classic Exploration of Faith in Community.* San Francisco, CA: HarperCollins, p. 98.
[20] Bonhoeffer, p. 99.
[21] *Ed. Note*: We did play ... he crushed me.

I have set you an example that you should do as I have done for you ... now that you know these things, you will be blessed if you do them. (John 13:15, 17).

Practical Action Step

So where do we begin this life of true servitude? I can think of no better launching point than the very words with which Foster closes his chapter on the discipline of service. So, I leave you with this:

The risen Christ beckons us to the ministry of the towel. Such a ministry, flowing out of the inner recesses of the heart, is life and joy and peace. Perhaps you would like to begin by experimenting with a prayer that several of us use. Begin the day by praying, "Lord Jesus, as it would please you bring me someone today whom I can serve."[22]

When He does (and I believe He will), serve faithfully.

---

[22] Foster, p. 140.

A Real Relationship

"Christina wants to know if you'll *go* with her."

I don't remember who the little girl was who stood in front of me in that moment, but I had the sense that I was about to make a life-changing decision in her midst. She'd been sent on a mission by her friend Christina – a mission to secure a boyfriend on the playground – and I was the target. As the friend waited in front of me, her eyes full of anticipation, I weighed out the pros and cons. Christina was pretty cute in my estimation, and I did know her a little, as we were on the same bus route. However, I was uncertain as to the public's perception of her;[1] but, she was a year older than I, so that couldn't hurt. Normally, this wasn't a tough call for me; I knew whom I liked and whom I didn't. But the request placed in Christina's name came out of left field, and I really needed to mull this over.

"I'm not sure," I said, cautiously. "Can I have a little time to think on it?"

"No, she kind of needs to know now."

Drats! Well-played, Christina's friend. I wasn't too sure on this one, but I wasn't exactly in position to be turning down boyfriend requests at that point in my life. My gut told me that it was a bit of a gamble, but my back was against the wall, as they say. "Yes," I finally said, probably with little enthusiasm. No sooner had I uttered that one word, than did her excited friend run back to Christina and give her the news, to which my new girlfriend responded by flashing me a sweet little smile. With that, I was in a serious relationship. We were *going together*.

Given my initial uncertainty about this relationship, the next couple of days weren't exactly a romantic whirlwind. When I

---

[1] Shamefully, a super-important criterion when you're … the age I was. I'll keep that number to myself.

thought it would help me, I told people I had a girlfriend. When I was uncertain of the response I'd get, I kept it to myself. Every now and then, someone would approach me and say, "I hear you are going with Christina!" Hesitantly, I would respond in the affirmative, waiting to see whether I'd be made fun of, or if they'd be impressed. I got a little of both during that time, but what really struck me was how quickly word got around. I spoke about it with several people with whom I normally didn't converse. In fact, over the course of that half-week, the only person I didn't really bump into was Christina herself.

They say that absence makes the heart grow fonder. Newsflash: sometimes it just makes you lose interest. And in the case of my playground romance, that is precisely what happened to me. Having come to the conclusion that this monumental decision I had made just a few days earlier had neither improved nor wrecked my life, I opted to move on. So I located Christina's anonymous friend and asked that she pass on the news: "Can you let Christina know I'm breaking up with her?"

"Sure," the girl replied, displaying far less interest than I had anticipated. And with that, our fairy-tale relationship was over.[2] It didn't last long, but I'll never forget the smile on her face when she heard that I said yes. Quite frankly, I *mustn't* forget that smile, because we didn't actually have any other memories to share. That was the only one. Throughout the course of our entire relationship, we never did speak to one another. To the best of my knowledge, of the handful of girlfriends I had as a kid, she alone holds that illustrious distinction.

Now, in light of that information, most reasonable grown-ups would be compelled to ask whether or not that was really a *relationship* at all. Granted, I did confirm that I was willing to be her boyfriend. And even though I didn't do it all the time, I did share my relationship status with a few people – usually only if they asked me, but still. So I *agreed* to be in a relationship, I *told others* I was in a relationship ... but in the absence of communication or interaction of any kind, could I really call it that?

Many of us would probably say no: what has been described above doesn't exactly meet the lowest threshold of what a personal relationship truly is. Yet, isn't it fascinating that many of us are perfectly content to adopt that same low standard when it comes to

---

[2] At least I'm assuming this is the case. Now that I think of it, I suppose I never bothered to confirm that the message was delivered. Oops.

what we describe as our *relationship* with God? We can perhaps remember the moment we said yes. Whether we knelt at an altar, raised our hand in a church service, prayed a prayer with a friend, or silently committed ourselves to God in private, we may remember the sensation that God was indeed smiling down on us right then. And over the course of days, months, maybe even years, we told a smattering of people about our relationship with Him. We didn't necessarily go out of our way most times, but if someone asked, we admitted our status: *yes, I am a Christian.*

But in the midst of that, any sense of real communication between us and the Lord is something of a foreign concept. Sure, we say a quick prayer before eating, and we may offer up an occasional plea for help when we encounter a problem we feel we can't handle on our own; but is that genuine communication? George Bernard Shaw once famously quipped, "The single biggest problem with communication is the illusion that it has taken place."[3] Thus, it may be necessary to ask ourselves, regarding our prayer lives, *has communication actually taken place? Does a relationship truly exist here?* That is, do we really *know* Him? Can we discern His voice when He speaks to us? And when He does, do we trust what He has to say?

Of all the truly fantastic events and themes of Scripture, I continue to be captivated by the mystery of the Incarnation. *That* Jesus walked among us as both *fully* God and *fully* man, I have no trouble believing; but any attempt of mine to explain precisely *how* these two natures were perfectly wed together in Him would likely prove inadequate. What particularly fascinates me in this regard is that He simultaneously offered to us both a perfect image of the Father,[4] as well as a portrait of what human beings can look like in relationship to God. Put another way, He showed us God, while at the same time, He showed us how to be related to God. And perhaps most notably, His example in the latter function was marked by a faithful life of prayer.

The Gospel writers inform us that Jesus spent the night praying to God prior to calling forth the Twelve (Luke 6:12). We are told that after a long night of healing the sick and exorcising demons,

---

[3] As quoted by Caroselli, M. (2000). *Leadership Skills for Managers*. New York, NY: McGraw-Hill, p. 71.
[4] See Colossians 1:15, along with John 14:7-11.

He found a solitary place, early in the morning, to seek the Father (Mark 1:35). We know that He would occasionally dismiss even His closest friends, that He might be alone in prayer (Mark 6:46); in fact, Luke reports that Jesus would often slip off alone into the wilderness to pray (Luke 5:16). He prayed early in the morning, and He was not opposed to praying through the night. He prayed before significant events, He prayed after them, and He prayed just because. Perhaps most memorably, He prayed for His followers (then and now) prior to His crucifixion (John 17), and when He reached the Garden of Gethsemane, He poured Himself out in prayer again (Mark 14:32-36).

In the midst of all He did over the course of those three years, the constant image placed before us is that of a praying man. Though He was God "in very nature," He was consumed by a longing to be in constant contact with the Father. Thus, I would contend that *to follow in His steps is to be a people devoted to the life of prayer*. Clearly, this was His expectation as He taught His followers about it:

> *And when you pray, do not be like the hypocrites, for they love to pray standing in the synagogues and on the street corners to be seen by men. I tell you the truth, they have received their reward in full. But when you pray, go into your room, close the door and pray to your Father, who is unseen. Then your Father, who sees what is done in secret, will reward you. And when you pray, do not keep on babbling like pagans, for they think they will be heard because of their many words. Do not be like them, for your Father knows what you need before you ask him.*
>
> *This, then, is how you should pray: "Our Father in heaven, hallowed be your name, your kingdom come, your will be done on earth as it is in heaven. Give us today our daily bread. Forgive us our debts, as we also have forgiven our debtors. And lead us not into temptation, but deliver us from the evil one." For if you forgive men when they sin against you, your heavenly Father will also forgive you. But if you do not forgive men their sins, your Father will not forgive your sins. (Matthew 6:5-15)*

I believe that one of the greatest hindrances to an intimate prayer life is the perception of ignorance. It's not that many of us don't *desire* a close relationship with the Lord – we just feel inadequate. Put another way, we simply don't know what to say or how to begin! My dream as a kid was not to have a girlfriend with whom I never spoke; I was just embarrassed and didn't know what to say to this girl. So, I opted for no communication. That's the way of playground romance, when you're a kid, I guess, but it's not the way of Jesus. The Father longs to communicate with you; Jesus showed us that in the life of a human being, such interaction is as vital as the air we breathe. And graciously, He did not leave us without a roadmap. In this critical passage, He teaches us what we need to know to walk in His steps: specifically, He offers us insights into *the heart* of prayer, *the purpose* of prayer, *the content* of prayer, and *the hindrances* to prayer.

The Heart of Prayer

As a child, whenever I heard more mature[5] Christians talk about the importance of a *prayer closet,* I always found myself very confused. The only *closet* with which I was familiar was a small, dark patch of real estate to the side of my room, and it smelled like shoes. It was where I tossed things that I didn't want to take the time to put away, so the thought of cramming myself in there for a time of intimate prayer didn't quite appeal to me. But as I got older myself and gained a better sense of the concept, I became infatuated with finding just the right spot for prayer.

As a college student, in particular, I traipsed all over campus in search of just the right place to get alone with God. I tried praying in my dorm room, but the constant intrusion of inexplicable noises and marginally sane peers made for a less-than-ideal devotional environment. I gave the campus chapel a try, but soon found that the cavernous space made me feel self-conscious. Outdoors was no good, as the incessant traffic of students proved to be a tremendous distraction. I then tried an isolated little building towards the middle of campus, but wasn't entirely certain I was allowed to be inside. Unfortunately, by the time I discovered a cozy little prayer room next to a handful of classrooms, I was ready to graduate and leave campus.

For some time after my tenure there, I continued to seek out that perfect locale in which I could know the Lord in a deeper way. What I would come to discover, however, is that the location of my

---

[5] Yep, I mean "old."

body was not nearly as critical as the positioning of my *heart*. For those of you who have found a treasured *prayer closet* of some sort, I say, good for you. There is nothing wrong with such a pattern; in fact, I too have come to adore a handful of quiet retreats over the years. But the thrust of our Lord's first instruction was not intended to serve as a geographical prohibition when it comes to prayer. Rather, what He sought to squelch in the listener was the sin of hypocrisy.

Notice that His teaching on prayer comes in the middle of a three-part instruction[6] on common Jewish acts of piety: alms-giving, prayer, and fasting. In each, He is contrasting His own guidance with the pattern of *hypocrites*, whose primary motivation in each act appears to be the praise of other men. In verses 5 and 6, then, He is neither forbidding public prayer nor demanding that all petitions be offered to God from behind closed doors.[7] Instead, He is calling the listener to genuine *intimacy* – not merely to a reputation of piousness.

D. A. Carson notes that "the public versus private antithesis is a good test of one's motives; the person who prays more in public than in private reveals that he is less interested in God's approval than in human praise."[8] Consider, for example, the minister exuding praise for his wife from the pulpit. When I preach, I tend to talk about my family quite a bit,[9] as I know no more practical and accessible fount of illustrations than my own life. And when I do, I am occasionally overcome with joy about something that God is teaching me through my precious wife. A by-product of this tendency is likely that most people in our congregation *assume* that she and I have a wonderful relationship. And as it happens, that is indeed the case. But imagine how my wife would respond to such public praise if, in private, I ignored her completely. Rather than beaming with joy at her husband's expression of love and gratitude, I would think that flattery in such a context would ring rather hollow. It may even elicit her anger. Put another way, if we lack true

---

[6] See Gaebelein, *The Expositor's Bible Commentary, Vol. 8.*, pp. 162ff for a fuller explanation.

[7] D. A. Carson adds, "if Jesus were forbidding all public prayer, then clearly the early church did not understand him (e.g., 18:19-20; Acts 1:24; 3:1; 4:24-30)." Ibid., p. 165.

[8] Ibid.

[9] Either with their permission or once they're out of the room. Just kidding.

relational intimacy, my expression of it in a public forum is mere hypocrisy.

Might I suggest that the same could be said of the Christian who rails against society and the government for "taking prayer out of our schools," for instance, while in her private life, prayer is no priority at all? Is it possible, do you suppose, that such hypocrisy incites the anger of our God? Again, the point of His first instruction is about what is at the heart of prayer: praying to God is not about ritual, it is not about location, nor is it even about a public-vs.-private setting. Ultimately, He is calling us to faithful *intimacy with the Father*, just as He Himself so clearly evidenced. Don't be like the hypocrites who want *people* to believe they're righteous, he said. Instead, privately seek the face of God, desiring only His approval. "Prayer," adds Maxie Dunnam, "is a personal relationship in which you and God move from a hello of politeness to an embrace of love."[10] Shut the door if you need to. Just find a way to enter His presence, that you might know Him, hear Him, and be transformed by Him.

The Purpose of Prayer

When I was a little boy, I was known to be a bit long-winded in my prayers. Surely my parents were thankful that I was *willing* to pray, but every now and again, I had to be gently persuaded to bring it to an "Amen." Regularly, as I sought the Lord's blessing on the food we were about to consume, I went ahead and mentioned every needy person who came to mind. Once I ran out of people, I moved on to our household possessions. Eventually, I found myself praying even for the table legs, which bravely held up our eating surface: go ahead and bless those too, Lord. Having heard countless lengthy prayers from pastors and laymen in my church, this was just about the only way I knew. I assumed that more words equated to better praying.

It seems, however, that children aren't the only ones to fall into that trap. How often do we pastors use our closing prayer as an opportunity to review the points of our sermon? Rather than simply seeking God's strength for obedience to all He's revealed to us, we instead opt to make sure that both God and man have another chance to soak in all our staggering insights! Or how about what I call the prayer name-droppers: *"Father God, we thank you, Father*

---

[10] Dunnam, M. (1998). *Unless We Pray: Brief Lessons on the Practice of Prayer.* Nashville, TN: Upper Room Books, p. 11.

God, for this chance to be here, Father God. And Father God, if you, Father God, could see fit, Father God, to give us another day, Father God, oh, Father God, we will serve you with it, Father God!" Do any of us talk like that normally? I mean, *ever?*

My purpose is not to poke fun at sincere pray-ers (I've definitely been guilty of both kinds, myself); but whether consciously or subconsciously, many of us have embraced the faulty notion that God is somehow impressed with our overabundance of words and/or our spiritual acumen. Consider again the words of Jesus: *And when you pray, do not keep on babbling like pagans, for they think they will be heard because of their many words. Do not be like them, for your Father knows what you need before you ask him.*

What He is telling us is that prayer is not about crafting the perfect literary statement. Prayer is not about putting my theology on display for God or for others. And it is certainly not about some sort of ritualistic repetition, which compels our Maker to listen more intently. We don't pray to impress anyone. We don't even pray to secure the favor of God. In fact, Jesus said that "your Father knows what you need before you ask." And in this fascinating statement, He gives us an insight into the primary reason that we adopt this particular means (prayer) in the pursuit of true intimacy with the Father.

Here is what I mean: I regard the above sentiment as fascinating, not because of its novelty – surely, we all could have easily surmised that an omniscient God knows our thoughts before they're spoken – but due to its primary implication. For, are we not now compelled to ask the following question: if God already knows what I need, then why bother speaking it in prayer? Why not just point to the heavens, give a nod ("you know my thoughts, God!"), and go on about our day?

Because the fact that God knows we need Him does not necessarily mean that you and I know the same. We do not pray to make God aware of our needs; we pray to confess our own awareness of our absolute dependence on Him. "In prayer we cease leaning on the staff of self-will and put all our confidence in God."[11] It always helps me to think of my own daughter at breakfast time. When she determines that she is hungry for cereal, every now and then she'll try to take care of it herself. I'll watch as she pulls the cereal from the pantry, climbs up on the countertop to reach the

---

[11] Dunnam, p. 99.

bowls, then I cringe as she attempts to drag the milk over to the pile of food she's poured out. I must admit, the entire process is a bit painful for me to watch, because at this point in her life, all she can really do on her own with a full jug of milk is to create a mess.

But then there are other days when she confesses her need for her dad's help. Even though very few words are spoken between us, she simply goes to the pantry, pulls out the box of cereal, and patiently waits for me to intervene. She doesn't fuss and fret and ask me over and over, because she knows it will be taken care of. Likewise, "prayer is a special exercise of faith. Faith makes the prayer acceptable because it believes that either the prayer will be answered, or that something better will be given instead."[12] Do you trust God with that measure of certainty when you pray? Like any father, God delights when His children crawl up into His lap and simply say, "I need you."

What He wants is your faith. What He wants is your recognition of full dependence on Him. He doesn't need your constant flow of words or your cleverly crafted statements; He calls for your childlike trust. Once we understand that and begin to submit our will to Him in all things, we enter the path of true intimacy with the Father. As I said, most of us don't enter into this relationship looking for something less than that; but, we nevertheless can find ourselves stuck for an entirely different reason: we just don't know what to say.

The Content of Prayer

Throughout my years in pastoral ministry, I have discovered that the easiest way to elicit terror in the hearts of many congregants is to ask them to pray in front of a group of people. Sometimes, just as a joke, I'll approach someone (who I know would be horrified at the very thought) just seconds before addressing the larger group, and I'll say, "I'm going to have you offer the prayer in just a moment." Then I quickly walk away. Usually, they find themselves speechless with their eyes wide and mouths agape for several seconds after I depart. Of course it's not healthy that I find humor in their fear. Yet, it serves as a reminder that many Christians, young and old, sense a distinct inadequacy when it comes to prayer.

Why is this so? Surely, for some, public speaking of any sort is the primary phobia. But what makes the prospect of public prayer

---

[12] Martin Luther, as quoted by Foster, R. & Smith, J. (1990). *Devotional Classics.* New York, NY: HarperCollins, p. 117.

so particularly daunting is that we really just don't know what to say to God. Our confusion, perhaps, comes from the mistaken notion that our prayer is only legitimate if it is completely original and generated spontaneously from the heart;[13] and ultimately, we are pretty sure we won't be able to craft something as beautiful as that evangelist we heard, or even our pastor. But this isn't at all what Jesus taught us.

As Carson astutely argues, when Jesus offered what has become known as "the Lord's Prayer," He gave us a *model* – not a strict form to be dutifully repeated: "This is *how* [not what] you should pray."[14] But in so doing, He graciously instructed His followers on the proper *content* of prayer. Rather than leaving us to our own imaginations, our Savior has set forth a clear pattern for us to follow as we present our petitions to the Father. Without question, countless biblical scholars throughout the ages have aptly navigated (and thoroughly explained) the specifics of this prayer. It may be helpful, though, to here offer a brief overview (verse-by-verse) of the particular categories taught by Christ.

(Verse 9) Our Father in heaven, hallowed be your name. Our prayers ought to begin with a clear understanding of whom it is we're addressing: our Father in heaven. "The first part of this suggests familiarity; the second demands reverence."[15] In other words, we have been taught to approach Him as we would a loving Father, confident in both His capacity to provide *and* in His love for us. But in so doing, we must not forget that He is the Almighty God of the universe. What is critical, however, is not so much that we follow the strict procedures of approaching deity, but that we rightly align our hearts and minds to the truth of who He is.[16] It is a *personal* address, which opens the door to genuine intimacy in communication.

---

[13] I wish I had more time to dig into this notion. For a fantastic treatment, check out Daniel Ethan Harris' *Live Prayerfully* (SalvationLife Books, 2013). He both explores and promotes praying with our own words, praying with no words, and praying with the words of others.

[14] Gaebelein, p. 169 (*emphasis mine*). Again, though, per Harris, this does not mean that there is something wrong with praying in these words. Carson's point is simply that they were never meant to serve as a linguistic constraint.

[15] Carter, p. 37.

[16] Gaebelein, p. 169.

Once the nature of the Father is clarified, Jesus then moves to the first of six petitions in this prayer. The first three deal with God and His honor, whereas the final three more directly address our own personal concerns.[17] Thus, He begins with the phrase, *hallowed be your name*. *Hallowed* is a word we do not commonly use today, but it is simply the verbal form of the word holy. To pray that God's name would be hallowed is effectively to seek that the name of the Lord be treated as holy.[18] Our first priority, upon addressing the Father, then, is to confess that He is worthy of all praise and honor; in a sense, it is still about aligning our hearts with Him.

(Verse 10) Your kingdom come, your will be done on earth as it is in heaven. The second and third requests, the establishment of both God's *kingdom* and His *will*, continue the theme of God's glory. Seeking His kingdom, of course, is both a *now* and *later* proposition. That is, when we pray that His kingdom will come, we are both petitioning for His reign to be established in our hearts now, as well as for the consummation of His kingdom at the "end of the age."[19] Similarly, when we call for His will to be done, we are praying that God's righteous decrees would be followed by the people.

These first three pleas, then, focus on the name, the kingdom and the will of the Father; nevertheless, they are "prayers that he may act in such a way that his people will hallow his name, submit to his reign, and do his will. It is therefore impossible to pray this prayer in sincerity without humbly committing oneself to such a course."[20] What we must take from this first section (the address with the initial petitions) is that prayer is not solely about our needs. Instead, we begin prayer by recognizing the Father and committing ourselves to His purposes in this world. Once we have, Jesus then shows us that there is indeed a place to seek God's provision for what we need.

(Verse 11) Give us today our daily bread. Of the final three requests, the first deals with our physical need for sustenance. This one is pretty straightforward, but take note of a few critical elements:[21] first, the request is made in the context of community. Just as the prayer is not offered to *my* Father, the request for bread is not made simply for *me*. This reminds us to look beyond just our

---

[17] Church, p. 1228.
[18] Gaebelein, p. 170.
[19] Ibid.
[20] Ibid., p. 171.
[21] Further expanded by Church, p. 1229.

own needs. Secondly, only bread is sought. We need not ask for frivolous extras, only what we need. Third, the petition is made only for what we need *today*. This is a tremendous reminder to renew our trust in Him every morning. Finally – and this one I particularly love – we ask that God would *give* it to us. Rather than serving as an open door to laziness or idleness, it is simply a recognition that we do not secure our own supply in this world. All we have is an absolute gift from God.

(Verse 12) Forgive us our debts, as we also have forgiven our debtors. Just as we need bread for the sustenance of our physical lives, we cannot obtain true spiritual life without the forgiveness of God. We need His mercy like we need daily food. What we cannot miss here, though, is the statement attached to this plea for forgiveness: *as we also have forgiven our debtors.* Charles Carter asserts that "for the professing Christian with an unforgiving spirit this is a dangerous prayer to repeat."[22] For, ultimately, we are asking the Lord to forgive us *to the same extent* that we have forgiven others. While some may struggle with the notion that our forgiveness is dependent on something that we *do* (that we somehow earn His forgiveness), C. F. D. Moule offers a helpful distinction. He "insists on distinguishing 'between, on the one hand, earning or meriting forgiveness, and, on the other hand, adopting an attitude which makes forgiveness possible.'"[23] Consider, then: would you be satisfied to seek forgiveness in the same measure you've been willing to give it to others? *All* others?

(Verse 13) And lead us not into temptation,[24] but deliver us from the evil one. For ages, readers have struggled to discern the appropriate meaning of this petition. Obviously, the Lord does not tempt us to sin (James 1:13-14). At the same time, we are taught to rejoice when *trials* (an acceptable alternative translation to "temptation" here) come our way (James 1:2). So what does this mean? Carson suggests that likely our best way to interpret this section is as a prayer for God to deliver us *through* the trials which come our way, keeping us from failure in the midst of them.[25]

In sum, then, these final three pleas teach us to seek God for that which we most acutely need for *whole* life: physical provision,

---

[22] Carter, p. 37.

[23] Gaebelein, p. 172.

[24] The Greek term here is πειρασμόν, which more often means "testing" than "enticement to sin." Ibid., p. 173.

[25] Ibid., pp. 173-174.

forgiveness, and the strength of God in the midst of trials and temptations. Thus, prayer is about drawing near to God in intimate fellowship, expressing our faith in Him, aligning our hearts and minds to His will, and asking Him to supply what only He can. This is the model we are given not only from the *teachings* of Jesus, but from His very life. So again, following Him means living as a prayerful people.

Hindrances to Prayer

I must confess, it would surely be great to end right there. The problem is, Jesus didn't. He closed this section by reiterating that, if we do not forgive others, forgiveness will not be granted to us. As I continued to reflect on those final words, I was reminded that a real commitment to prayer – like that of our Lord – is not simply about the time we are willing to set apart for devotions. *Living a life devoted to prayer is about being the kind of people whose prayers will be heard.* Therefore, we need to pay close attention to the testimony of Scripture, where it speaks on that very issue. While this list is not exhaustive, I do want to highlight three such hindrances to effective prayer.

First, as has already been mentioned, our prayers for *forgiveness* will not be heard when we refuse to offer it to those who have offended us. I have dealt with this at length in an earlier chapter, but it is worth noting again that our willingness to extend grace over the sins of others probably provides a keen insight into our comprehension of our own guiltiness. Secondly, God declared through the prophet Isaiah that a *poor treatment of the weak* will prompt God to "hide [His] eyes from you; even if you offer many prayers, [He] will not listen" (Isaiah 1:15-17). When we neglect (or directly oppress) the poor and the broken, God turns His ears from our prayers. Finally, Peter taught that our prayers can be hindered by our *failure to love and submit to one another in the home*.[26] We often act as if our faithfulness to the Lord is somehow disconnected from our patterns of treating our children, parents, spouse, etc. But the message here is clearly that what we do and how we love at home directly impacts our level of intimacy with the Lord.

Is there anything hindering your prayer life? Are there attitudes and activities in your life that do not belong? Regardless of how faithful you are in setting aside time for prayer, you may need

---

[26] See 1 Peter 3:7. The statement is made to husbands, specifically, but the context suggests that it is true for all such relationships.

the sober reminder today that God does not choose to listen to all of us.[27] When we pepper Him with all our wants and desires without first honoring Him – not only with our words, but also with the very trajectory of our lives – He has made it clear that He will not respond. If God does not seem to be inhabiting your prayers today, perhaps your first step should be to examine yourself, honestly seeking the full cleansing of the Lord.

Some of us are hindered in prayer because of our own sin. Others of us struggle to pray, perhaps because we don't understand the purpose. We don't understand the point of speaking words to an invisible God who knows them already. Still others of us feel stunted in prayer, simply because we're not sure *what* to say. We know we're not eloquent, we know our theology needs some work; so we often opt for little to no communication at all, rather than struggling through what is perhaps uncomfortable at first. To you I would say this: what God wants is *you*. He is not interested in your big words, He doesn't need for you to impress others with your powerful prayers ... He just wants you to climb up into His arms, confess your need for Him, and rest in the confidence that He is willing and able to meet your needs. It may not be in the manner which you'd prescribe, but He longs for you to trust in His goodness and wisdom, as a child does with her dad.

Jesus showed us what it looks like to maintain true intimacy with the Father. And through His example of a life committed to prayer, He reminded us that a real relationship demands the intimacy of genuine, two-way communication. Anything less is merely a playground romance.

Practical Action Step

Undoubtedly, we will each approach this chapter from a different starting point. We will likely range from no prayer life at all, to multiple devotional hours each day, and everywhere in between. But the good news is that we can all experience a greater depth of intimacy with Him than what we have today. So wherever your starting point may be, allow me to offer two simple strategies through which we can invite the Lord to draw us closer to Him.

---

[27] Again, let us be clear about who this is. I am not talking about a sincere person who believes him- or herself to be "un-hearable" due to past sin. The reader should take this statement only within the context specified above.

First, take some time now to ask the Father to reveal to you any hindrances in your prayer life. I've highlighted three above, but perhaps there are others He wants to speak to you. Ask Him if your relationships at home and at work/school are all glorifying to Him. Invite Him to peer into your private life, your habits, and your treatment of the weak. Ask Him to show you if there is an unforgiving spirit in you.

Secondly, write out and/or memorize the Lord's Prayer (if you haven't already), and spend time praying slowly through each verse. Take time to reflect on God's glory and His love for you. Be intentional about bending your will to His, praying that His Kingdom would take hold of you and others. Lift up in prayer those who are far from Him now. And as you present your needs, seek His provision not only in the physical, but in the spiritual as well. Be specific, and make sure you don't do all the speaking!

Remain in Me

"You people do realize that swindlers and hookers are entering God's Kingdom ahead of you, right?"

That's got to hurt, no matter who you are. But when you're the premier religious authorities of your people, and Jesus says this to you in front of everyone who is gathered in the temple courts, I have to believe that these words come with added bite. It would have been humiliating enough had He just said it without warning – but Jesus added salt to the wound by first getting them to admit as much themselves.

"What do you think?" he asked them. "There was a man who had two sons. He went to the first and said, 'Son, go and work today in the vineyard.' 'I will not,' he answered, but later he changed his mind and went. Then the father went to the other son and said the same thing. He answered, 'I will, sir,' but he did not go. Which of the two did what his father wanted?"[1]

The chief priests and the elders couldn't help but give the obvious answer: the first son, of course. But no sooner did they respond, than Jesus illuminated the implications of their own confession. You guys are the ones who talk about faithfulness to the Father. You guys are the ones with the reputation for strict adherence to the Law. You guys are the ones claim to do His will. But when John (the Baptist) came and showed you what righteousness really is, you rejected him. But these ones didn't. All these lost souls – these cast-offs known only for their rampant immorality – they didn't make that mistake. Though they've rejected righteousness and sinned against the Father in a myriad of ways, they're the ones who turned and responded in humble *obedience*. They're the ones entering God's kingdom and actually pleasing Him; you know ... just like you admitted a minute ago.

---

[1] Matthew 21:28-31.

Like I said, *humiliating*. But how much more so should this story be for some of us today? The elders and the chief priests of Israel should have known better, of course; but, you and I have the benefit of the whole of Christ's teaching – not to mention the abiding and empowering presence of the Holy Spirit. Of all people throughout history, we ought to be crystal clear on what it is that pleases the Father. And yet, *obedience* remains a rather unpopular word. Now, we don't mind talking about *faith* or *belief*; those are words with which we're relatively comfortable, but mostly because we have relegated them to the conviction of our minds and the confession of our tongues. That is, we don't mind agreeing with theological statements, or even admitting to others that we do. We're just not so sure we want to change our lifestyle to reflect those convictions. And to be honest, some of us aren't quite convinced that we *need* to.

After all, the apostle Paul taught that we have been saved by grace through faith, did he not? That it is a gift of God, not secured by our works, so that no one can boast.[2] So if that's the case, then our salvation isn't dependent on our obedience! All we need to do, we tell ourselves, is to believe the facts He told us to believe, and His grace will cover the rest. Some of us even look down our noses at those in the church who tout purity, suggesting that they are simply Pharisees, bound by a legalistic illusion. *I'm not perfect*, we boast, *but God accepts me because He loves me!*

OK. But we struggle a bit when we argue from that position, don't we, to deal with the command to be *perfect* as our heavenly Father is perfect (Matthew 5:48)? Or to be holy in *all* you do (1 Peter 1:15)? Unfortunately, such a response tends to come as a reaction to the opposite approach, which really isn't any better. On the other side of the pew are those who slavishly (and joylessly) follow the rules as though we're working towards a good grade. We sing, "I'm so happy, so very happy, I've got the love of Jesus in my heart;" but when our brow is furrowed, our shoulders are drooped and our head is down, it looks more like we're singing to convince ourselves.

A lot of us can see the irony in either of those extremes, however. So where most of us choose to land is in that nebulous realm of *selective obedience*. We obey the commands with which we're comfortable, but we turn our faces from His when purity costs too much. Effectively, we sit in judgment over the Scripture,

---

[2] See Ephesians 2:8-9.

deciding which parts of it He *really* meant. We wouldn't admit to doing that, of course, but the pattern of our lives indicates otherwise. We follow Him wholeheartedly when it comes to loving the disenfranchised, for instance, but we neglect His call to sexual purity. Or, we make sure never to say any unwholesome words, but we gossip unashamedly about our brothers and sisters in Christ. Does this seem like a better alternative?

Admittedly, I've spent time at all three stations. What I have found, however, is that not one of them led to genuine peace and joy in Christ. The problem, it seems to me, is that we often regard these three patterns as our only options, when it comes to obedience. But I would submit to you that Jesus calls us to something entirely different:

> *I am the true vine, and my Father is the gardener. He cuts off every branch in me that bears no fruit, while every branch that does bear fruit he prunes so that it will be even more fruitful. You are already clean because of the word I have spoken to you. Remain in me, and I will remain in you. No branch can bear fruit by itself; it must remain in the vine. Neither can you bear fruit unless you remain in me. I am the vine; you are the branches. If a man remains in me and I in him, he will bear much fruit; apart from me you can do nothing. If anyone does not remain in me, he is like a branch that is thrown away and withers; such branches are picked up, thrown into the fire and burned. If you remain in me and my words remain in you, ask whatever you wish, and it will be given to you. This is to my Father's glory, that you bear much fruit, showing yourselves to be my disciples.*

> *As the Father has loved me, so have I loved you. Now remain in my love. **If you obey my commands, you will remain in my love, just as I have obeyed my Father's commands and remain in his love.** I have told you this so that my joy may be in you and that your joy may be complete. My command is this: Love each other as I have loved you. Greater love has no one than this, that he lay down his life for his friends. You are my friends if you do what I command. I no longer call you servants, because a servant does not know his master's business. Instead, I have called you friends, for everything that I learned from my Father I have made known to you. You did*

*not choose me, but I chose you and appointed you to go and bear fruit – fruit that will last. Then the Father will give you whatever you ask in my name. This is my command: Love each other. (John 15:1-17, **emphasis mine**)*

The clear indication is that *to follow Jesus is to walk in complete obedience to His commands*. Nonexistent or selective obedience is neither the pattern He modeled for us, nor is it the expectation He has for His disciples. Simultaneously, there is no hint of joyless, dutiful adherence here, either; instead, He describes a fulfilling, joyful life of abiding with Him in love. He paints a picture of obedience that is a life-giving delight – a participation in the communion which He shares with the Father. So how do we get there? Over the course of this chapter, I want to explore with you the *results*, the *source*, and the *secret* to obedience. But first, let us strengthen this foundation by making clear His primary instruction.

The Words We Cannot Avoid
"Daddy, can I run next door?"

"No, I want you to stay with me," I told my 6-yr-old daughter.

"Pleeeeaaaase!" she begged. "I want to say goodbye to my friend!"

"Honey, the answer is no. You will see her again in a couple days, and she's probably left already anyway. Stay right here." As near as I could tell, those were clear instructions. Or at least I thought so, until I turned my head to walk into the kitchen and I heard the front door slam shut behind her. She was halfway across the yard when I opened the door and hollered her name. With the sternest tone I could muster, I instructed her to get back inside – a command she wisely obeyed this time. And when she sheepishly entered the house, she found herself in a lot of trouble. So much so, that she called my own mother the next day to see if she'd be willing to punish me in like manner.

There are times when I cut my kids some slack, because I recognize that perhaps they didn't understand what they were asked to do. This was not one of those times: I could not have made my expectations any clearer to my little girl. When it comes to the expectation of Jesus that His followers would live in full obedience to His commands, the same is most certainly true: there is not much else He could have said. Consider His statements in this passage

118

alone: *if you obey my commands, you will remain in my love* (v. 10); *you are my friends if you do what I command* (v. 14).

Straightforward, right? The same is true when we begin to broaden the context. In the previous chapter, He declared the following: *if you love me, you will obey what I command* (14:15); *whoever has my commands and obeys them, he is the one who loves me* (14:21); *if anyone loves me, he will obey my teaching* (14:23); *he who does not love me will not obey my teaching* (14:24). As we expand even further, we recognize that such obedience was the expectation of God from the very beginning of His covenant with the nation of Israel. For instance: *If you pay attention to these laws and are careful to follow them, then the Lord your God will keep his covenant of love with you, as he swore to your forefathers* (Deut. 7:12).

It should be clear to those familiar with the Scripture, of course, that the death and Resurrection of Jesus ushered in the New Covenant. Nevertheless, the expectation of obedience to the Lord's commands remained unchanged even after His ascension: *No one who is born of God will continue to sin, because God's seed remains in him; he cannot go on sinning, because he has been born of God* (1 John 3:9). The reason, of course, as Paul points out to the Galatians, is that our righteousness was never secured by the Law in the first place. Even then, Abraham's righteousness was credited to him by the very same grace of God, received through his trust in the Lord.[3] Thus, even when the Law was given, it was ultimately pointing ahead to Christ and His sacrifice. Let it suffice to say for now, though, that this call to obedience has *always* existed at the heart of our relationship to God. No matter where we look or how we seek to interpret the text, the unavoidable reality is that our Lord expects us to walk in full obedience to Him; in fact, that kind of life is central to who He made us to be.

The Results of Obedience

Isn't it a wonderful feeling to be *chosen*? When I was a junior in high school, I ran cross country with the distinct sense that I had been chosen. One day the previous spring, when I was out practicing for a track meet, the cross-country coach approached me for a private conversation. We'd never spoken before, but somehow he knew my name. "Ryan," he said, "I would like for you to consider running cross country in the fall. I think you'd be really good at it

---

[3] See Galatians 3:6ff.

and I'd love to have you on the team." As soon as he said it, I was beaming. I wasn't sure what it was about my mediocre 100m hurdling that made him think I could capably run a 5k, but I didn't care. No coach in any sport had ever said anything like that to me ... ever. I had no desire to run that distance, but I sure did want to be wanted.[4]

It is probably fair to suggest that the same desire lies deep within all of us: we want someone to choose us – for the team, for marriage, for a prize, it doesn't matter. We just want to be selected, because it somehow feels like a validation of who we are. When it's a cross-country coach who mysteriously knows your name, it feels pretty great. How much more so, then, when it is the Lord of all creation? Throughout this passage, Jesus reveals that our obedience doesn't just *satisfy* the Father; rather, it produces two significant results, both of which ought to bring delight to the believer. And the first one we'll examine stems from the knowledge that we were chosen by Christ for a purpose.

You did not choose me, but I chose you and appointed you to go and bear fruit – fruit that will last. As Jesus looked intently into the eyes of His beloved apostles, He reminded them that they had been selected. Notice that this conversation with them is happening shortly before His arrest and crucifixion. This is likely an incredibly difficult and emotional time for them all, and so Jesus takes the time to remind them of their worth: they were selected by the Messiah! But this selection was not meant to simply serve as a source of pride; rather, He reminded them that they were *chosen for a purpose.* Specifically, that they would go out from Him and bear lasting fruit. The same is surely true of you and me.

The first critical result of obedience, then, is that in bearing such fruit (following His commands), *we fulfill the purpose for which we were created and redeemed.* For a people who seem to be obsessed with our purpose in life, this ought to come as rather refreshing news. Because, the fact is, no one wants to fail to live up to his or her purpose.

---

[4] Once the season began, I discovered why he wanted me so badly on the team: I was a male. There were only two other guys who ran, and he wanted to field some semblance of a boys' team. I can only assume he had the same "I-think-you'd-be-great" talk with half a dozen other runners that spring. That sound you hear is my ego deflating.

At the time of writing, I have been serving as the pastor of Trinity Chapel for nearly six years. And from the day I first walked into my office, I've had a pencil sharpener on my desk. It's a fancy little gizmo – with a sleek design – from a well-known electronics shop. It doesn't need to be plugged in, but neither am I required to do any work, like with those old hand-crank versions.[5] I just gently insert the pencil, and out comes a magically sharpened writing utensil. Or at least I assume that's what *should* happen. Because in six years, I've yet to have it sharpen my pencil. Admittedly, for the first couple of years, I just ignored it. I don't use a lot of pencils, thus negating my need for a sharp one. But after a while, I thought I'd give it a try. When it responded by doing nothing, I thought, no problem. It must just need a battery. So I dutifully replaced the power source and gave it another try.

This time, it started churning as soon as my pencil passed the entrance. But once I tried to make said pencil come into contact with the blades, it stopped working. Several times I tried this, with minor adjustments each time. And in every instance, the sharpener shut down on contact, as my dull pencil remained dull. Shortly before losing my mind, I finally gave up on my fancy pencil sharpener. But as I reflected on my experience, I began to ask this question: do I really have a *pencil sharpener* on my desk? I mean, it looks like a pencil sharpener. Per the writing on the unit, it purports to sharpen pencils; yet, no matter how many times I've tried, it has yet to produce a sharpened pencil. So, effectively, I have a thing on my desk that calls itself (and looks like) a pencil sharpener, but I'm not so sure it *is* one. For – and correct me if I'm wrong – a pencil sharpener sharpens pencils!

Can we be reminded that we weren't chosen by Christ just so that we could call ourselves Christians? He didn't rescue us from eternal damnation just so that we could sit somewhere and claim to be His followers. He called us out and raised us up *so that* we would go and bear lasting fruit. He called us out for a life of genuine obedience! And when we live in full submission to *all* He has taught us, we fulfill the purpose for which we were chosen, *showing ourselves to be the disciples of Christ* (v. 8). When we do not ... well, is it possible that we're not what we claim to be? Eventually, I threw out my "pencil sharpener." Likewise, Jesus soberly declared that the Father "cuts off every branch in me that bears no fruit" (v. 2).

---

[5] Yes, I'm talking about a battery-powered pencil sharpener. So I'm easily impressed – big deal.

So, first, our obedience leads to the fulfillment of our purpose, giving us true identity. It shows us to be who we say we are. But Jesus further pointed out that it's not just about us: *the second result of bearing much fruit is that it glorifies the Father* (v. 8). It is in this, I would argue, that we find genuine communion with Christ. For, as He Himself would declare just a couple chapters later, glorifying the Father was the culmination of His own work on earth. "I have brought you glory on earth by completing the work you gave me to do," He said, as He prayed for Himself, shortly before facing the cross.[6] Could we say as much today? Have our lives brought glory to God?

Clearly, the two results are related: it is to God's glory that His people fulfill their purpose. It causes others to take note of our transformed and purposeful lives, which then enables them to believe that God can truly be trusted to set us free in this life. In a sense, our fulfillment is His glory, and His glory is our fulfillment. Thus, again, our eyes are being drawn to something deeper than joyless servitude; instead, Jesus is painting for us a picture of what it looks like to participate in the communion which He shares with the Father.

The Source of Obedience

> I am the vine; you are the branches. If a man remains in me and I in him, he will bear much fruit; apart from me you can do nothing (v. 5).

Quick, raise your hand if you remember Marty McFly and the Flux Capacitor. In 1985, right about the time I was first able to remember and sit through a film, my mom took me to see *Back to the Future*. If there was a cooler 80's teen than Marty McFly, I never found him. Everything he was, I wanted to be; in fact, I picked up a childhood interest in skateboarding and electric guitar-playing just because of him.

If you're unfamiliar with the movie, the plot centers around time travel and the effects it can exert on future events. Shortly before the teenage McFly travels back in time in the DeLorean designed by his eccentric friend, Dr. Emmett Brown, the Doctor explains the one element of the car which is absolutely critical to

---

[6] John 17:4.

time travel: the *flux capacitor*. Though it's unclear as to precisely how this Y-shaped lamp-in-a-box enables a DeLorean to move from 1985 to 1955, Doc Brown is adamant about one thing: "This is what makes time travel possible." We don't know how *it* works, we just know that time travel doesn't work without *it*.

Likewise, the underlying theme of this passage in John reveals a critical truth which we cannot miss: *without an intimate union with Jesus, obedience doesn't work*. He begins this section with a profound metaphor: He is the vine, and we are the branches. As long as the branches are connected to the vine, they have life and can bear fruit. "No branch," He says, "can bear fruit by itself; it must remain in the vine" (v. 4). In the same way, when we are not connected with Him – abiding in Him, and He in us – we cannot bear genuine fruit.

Think for a moment about the implications of that statement. First, the good news is that obedience is not simply about following orders as an act of thanks for what He did for us on the cross. It is staggering how often this has been taught in our churches: that obedience is what we do in response to what He did. On its face, that probably doesn't sound so bad; and in a certain (limited) sense, I suppose it is true. We do choose to obey, and we do so gladly because of His love for us. The problem, however, is that such a description of obedience leads us to believe that we, by the strength of our own will power, are sent out to do good deeds because we're grateful.

We need only observe the same dynamic between two people to realize that this is a short-lived phenomenon. Think about the last time someone did something heroically sacrificial for you. Maybe they gave you an amazing gift, forgave you a terrible offense, or did some other spectacular act of kindness. I imagine that, for a while, you were willing to do anything for that person. You'd adjust your schedule, give up your own comfort, whatever they needed. But before long, you got to the place where you felt like the two of you were probably about even. And because of that, the sense of awe and gratitude that once drove you to move heaven and earth for her, had now waned considerably. Pretty soon, even the smallest request from your benefactor seemed like a lot to ask.

Sadly, the same thing happens when we regard obedience solely as a display of gratitude. Before long, our remorse over sin runs low, we convince ourselves that we probably weren't that bad in the first place, and a few months of really good deeds probably ought to make you square with the Lord. After that, obedience can become wearisome, and the demands seem tyrannical. However, when we understand obedience as the fruit of an intimate relationship with Him, the entire dynamic changes. Of course we still choose it, and of course we still do so because of the depth of His love. But we are no longer slaving away somewhere on our own, driven by a sense of gratitude.

Instead, we are both inspired and empowered by His presence within us. Knowing Him becomes more central than following rules; yet, the more we know of Him, the more He transforms us. The more we are filled with His Spirit, the more His nature spills out of us. In this sense, our obedience becomes less about what we do, and more about what He is doing in us. It is less our response to Him than it is the fruit of His activity in us.

First, then, our obedience is a result of His abiding presence; but secondly, if this indeed the case, then we must also admit that when we are apart from the vine, we cannot produce the type of fruit He desires. Put another way, our "good works" are not acceptable to the Father when they are not generated by Christ in us. Lots of people, Christian or not, can perform deeds which would be compatible with Christian values. Anyone can feed the hungry, fight for justice, and even sacrifice for another. But as John Wesley deftly argues, goodness is not merely an objective category; rather, it is a descriptor for the nature of God. Therefore, any works which are produced apart from His nature cannot be found truly pleasing in His sight.[7]

In short, the only source for God-pleasing obedience is Christ Himself. This is both an encouragement and a warning: on the one hand, we are not being compelled to simply muster up enough thanksgiving to follow all the rules; on the other hand, neither can we merit His favor by doing good works on our own. His call to obedience is, primarily, an invitation to live in perfect fellowship and communion with Him. And in this light, He reveals the beautiful secret of living in obedience to the Father ...

The Secret of Obedience

Admittedly, to refer to it as a secret makes it sound like He's hiding something from us. Nothing could be further from the truth. Nevertheless, I have found this truth to be *secretive* in the sense that

---

[7] Wesley, J., *Sermon 5: Justification by Faith*. From *The Works of John Wesley, Vol. 5* (Reprinted in 2007). Grand Rapids, MI: Baker Books.

too many of us have yet to hear and fully embrace it. Hopefully, the trajectory of this chapter has so far been pointing us in this direction, but it needs to be stated nonetheless. In my humble opinion, the secret of obedience is simply this: your works do not earn you the love of God; *you are loved already.*

As the Father has loved me, so have I loved you. Now remain in my love (v. 9). My friend Tony once incited my jealousy by sharing with me an experience from his days in grad school. He was enrolled in a class with a professor who opted for a somewhat unique approach to learning. Whereas most of his colleagues seemed to take delight in making the students sweat out the learning process, this teacher took another route. On the first day of class, Tony told me, his professor made a statement that changed the entire dynamic of the course. When the students gathered around him for the first time, he looked them all in the eyes and said this: "everyone in here already has an A for the course. Now let's buckle down and enjoy the learning." With the stress of performance removed, the class engaged in what proved to be the most fascinating and compelling course of his entire program.

Tony shared this with me in the midst of my own graduate program, and it made my heart sing.[8] For most of my life, I've been obsessed with performing well. With school in particular, while some of my friends were out having a good time, I was inside studying. When others would give it a shot and be satisfied with the results, I was meticulously scanning over every answer, every word, to see to it that I would be graded well. Some would probably regard this as a positive quality. But as I've had opportunity to look deep within my own heart, I've come to recognize that this pattern has generated from a rather unhealthy need: through performance, I've been trying to validate my worth. That is, if I can win, score highly, or be perfect, then I matter. I am worthy of someone's love.

I still remember the day when God revised my thinking. I was sitting on my couch in Pittsburgh, with my head hung low before the Lord. I had disappointed Him yet again, and I was certain that He was fed up with me. Completely dejected, I told God that I would understand if He was done with me. I just couldn't get it right, and so I'm probably not worth the time. No sooner did those words enter my mind, than was this phrase spoken deep into my heart: "Ryan, don't you know how much I love you?" It came so suddenly and so

---

[8] The title of my song? "I'm so jealous I could throw a punch."

125

clearly, that I knew it was from the Lord. As I let those words resonate within my soul, tears began to form in my eyes. Then more tears chased them out, and before long I was weeping. Because despite the fact that I'd grown up in church and had heard a thousand times that *Jesus loves me*, the truth was, I didn't know.

Or maybe I should say, up until that point, I didn't believe it. I was sure that all my efforts were securing for me the love of my Father; I was convinced that He would treasure me *if* I was good enough. But in that moment on my couch, He held me close and made perfectly clear the depth of His free gift of love. And for the first time, I understood what Jesus was telling us all along: *just as the Father has loved me (eternally), I have loved you.* You didn't earn it, nor *will* you with what I'm about to say. It's already been given – now remain in me, choose to remain in that love, by living in obedience.

Now, don't be alarmed. I am not here suggesting some sort of universalism where everyone's already promised heaven, now do your best to obey out of the goodness of your heart! I don't believe the Scripture allows for that in the least. What I am saying is that you're not starting from zero, working towards the elusive love of God. You already have it. He loved you even in the depth of your sin. He is beckoning you, rooting for you, pleading that you will remain in what has been given to you – not by merit, but by His matchless grace. You have nothing to prove. Just enjoy His love by allowing Him to produce righteousness in you.

Obey My Commands

So what does this abiding look like? Quite simply, it is about loving Him in return. And as we saw above, Jesus painted a clear picture of what that means in chapter 14: "If anyone loves me, he will obey my teaching. My Father will love him, and we will come to him and make our home with him. He who does not love me will not obey my teaching."[9] What, then, is the content of His teaching? Of course, what follows is not exhaustive, but I always find the Sermon on the Mount[10] to be good place to begin asking ourselves this question: *am I living in obedience to what He taught?*

That is, Jesus said that we're to be light shining into a darkened world. Am I letting my light shine in the darkest places? He taught that if there is a conflict between me and my brother, I

---

[9] John 14:23-24a.
[10] See Matthew 5:13 – 7:6 for the source of the following two paragraphs.

ought to lay down what I am offering to God and go things right. Am I living at peace with all others? He made clear that to lust after another person is to commit adultery. Are my eyes drinking in what does not belong to me? Are my thoughts remaining pure? Jesus said that my speech ought to be simple and my commitments ought to be honored: in marriage, to others, and to Him. Am I a man of my word? He taught that I must reject vengeance and hatred towards enemies – that I must love in the same way He has loved. Am I faithful in that?

He commanded that I give to those in need, cling to Him in prayer, and eschew food from time to time, that I might lean solely on His provision; He said that in all these things, I must refuse to seek glory from others. Am I content to sacrifice and to please Him alone? Jesus said that I ought to have a healthy view of possessions in this world, refusing to serve and treasure them as I do Him. Is my heart free from greed, and my devotion to Him singular? He taught that there is no place for worry in the life of a believer. Do I entrust all things to His care? He made clear that I am not the judge of my fellow man. Do I faithfully leave that to Him as well?

Again, the point is not to slavishly work through a checklist when it comes to obedience. But neither should we speak vaguely about the teaching of Jesus: it's all before us if we're interested to look. That said, He certainly is willing to put it all in a nutshell for us, isn't He? In the passage before us, He makes reference to His commands, many of which I've outlined above; but, that doesn't keep Him from narrowing our focus. *My command is this: Love each other as I have loved you.* Love others enough to offer them the word of life, to live peacefully with them, to be faithful and honest to them, to sacrifice and submit to them, just as Jesus showed us. In so doing, we reflect the love of our Savior. In so doing, we choose to remain in the love that has already been so graciously poured out for us.

The life of obedience is not about repaying a debt. It's not about earning the love of the Father. Jesus said, the Triune God wants to make His home in your heart. Remain in me, let my Spirit fill you, and the resultant fruit will be the kind of life that brings glory to God.

In one of my favorite books, *In His Steps*, author Charles Sheldon describes a church service that was interrupted by a homeless man with a pressing question. What the church *said* about herself did not seem to match up with what he was seeing from her, amidst the harsh realities of life on the street. In the silence of the stunned congregation, he made this comment:

> *I heard some people singing at a church prayer meeting the other night, "All for Jesus, all for Jesus, all my being's ransomed powers, all my thoughts, and all my doings, all my days, and all my hours," and I kept wondering as I sat on the steps outside just what they meant by it. It seems to me there's an awful lot of trouble in the world that somehow wouldn't exist if all the people who sing such songs went and lived them out.*[11]

Indeed. Let us be a people not satisfied merely with the *reputation* for obedience. Instead, in every way, as we love God and our neighbor in the strength of the Spirit, let us choose to remain in Him by following in the steps of Jesus.

Practical Action Step

Did you notice that the word "remain" appears eleven times in the first ten verses of John 15:1-17?[12] We are called to remain in Him, remain in His love, and to allow His words to remain in us. As it has hopefully become clear by this point, obedience is not simply something we choose to go and do. Rather, it is the fruit which comes as a result of connectedness to the Lord. So perhaps the place to get started is with an intentional effort to remain in His teaching. If you do not currently make a regular practice of reading the Scripture, begin doing so today. Do not feel the need to take on enormous chunks at a time; read for understanding rather than rapid completion. And in light of what we've explored together here, start out in the Gospels (Matthew, Mark, Luke and John), that you might be exposed immediately to all that Jesus taught.

If you already are in the Scripture regularly (or, *once you are*), try doing something similar to what I did above with the Sermon on the Mount: jot down the commands He gave and begin to examine your own life to see whether or not you are faithfully walking in obedience to what He said. And if you encounter teaching which you have thus far failed to follow, choose to make a change this very day, knowing that you are deeply loved and that God will gladly give you all the strength you need.

---

[11] Sheldon, C. (1967), *In His Steps*. Grand Rapids, MI: Zondervan, p. 9.
[12] To be precise, all appearances occur in verses 4-10.

Sheep and Goats

His name was Ronnie,[1] and his eyes told me right away that he was mischievous. He was one of the first teens I met when I came home to serve the church of my youth. At the time, he was nearing graduation, and wasn't exactly a regular at church anymore ... but he used to be, I was told. He was a nice kid, looking to connect, and looking to keep himself out of trouble; to be honest, I'd not met very many kids who seemed that aware of their own weaknesses. Like I said, I didn't see Ronnie every week, but once every couple of months he would show up, and I would go out of my way to let him know how good it was to see him there.

When he finally graduated, I knew that his newfound freedom probably wouldn't be great for him. But never in a million years did I expect to wake up to the news I did on that spring morning: police had caught Ronnie hiding in a field near his home, and they believed he had just fired the shot which killed his own father. Big Ron was a local hero. He'd served as an officer on the fire department in a small rural community. He was a gregarious guy, known and beloved by everyone in town. At home, though, he was old-school. He was a firm disciplinarian, and he and the mischievous Ronnie didn't always see eye-to-eye.

Unfortunately, on the previous night, Ronnie and his dad had been arguing out by the barn. The story, though unconfirmed, was that Ronnie had taken some drugs into his system. And coupled with pent up frustration at his strict father, he finally lost it. None of us will ever know what was said between the two of them that night in the yard, but what we do know is that Ronnie picked up a shot gun and fired it right at his father's head. Big Ron was killed instantly. When I went out to their home later that morning with two of my

---

[1] Fake name alert!

colleagues, we just wanted to comfort Ronnie's sister and mother. I had no idea what I'd say or do, we just figured we ought to be there. They were obviously hurting, but the event was so shocking and fresh, it hadn't really sunk in yet. While they'd clearly lost their husband and father, they were also grieving the fact that they had [effectively] lost their son and brother, as well. Imagine a mother hurting so badly for her son who was in trouble, yet simultaneously being forced to come to grips with the fact that he'd murdered her husband. I couldn't imagine.

What was clear to me that day, however, was that my place was not only to minister to the younger sister, but also to Ronnie himself. Though he'd committed this horrific crime, he still needed someone to reach out to him. When I told his mother that I planned to see him, she seemed thankful. Mostly because she knew she wouldn't be able to see him herself just yet. I was in my early 20s at the time, and going to see this young man seemed like a noble thing to do, in my mind. But as I left the house that day, my heart began to tremble inside me. I'd never been inside any sort of jail before (that I could remember), let alone to visit a murderer. Fear swept over me, and I began to wonder what I'd say – or what he'd say.

My friend Jeff (our middle school pastor) graciously agreed to join me, and we got in within the next day or so. Ronnie was being held temporarily at the county jail, and once we cleared the security checks, they walked us into a room about the size of a bathroom. We sat on one bench, and he would be led to the other. When they brought him in, his face was red from at least a full day of crying. Those mischievous eyes had been replaced by a look of deadness. He was in shock over what he'd done, and he could barely bring himself to speak. His eyes were watery, his nose was running ... this kid was an absolute mess. Truth be told, I don't remember quite what we said in our few minutes together. I think we asked him how he was holding up, shared with him that God had not abandoned him, and that neither had we. He seemed to appreciate it all, but it was still difficult for him to process the whole thing.

As we said goodbye and walked out of there, tears began to well up in my own eyes. My heart broke for that entire family. But more than anything, I just knew that I never wanted to set foot in there again. I felt inadequate, fearful, and I was consumed by pain. What I wanted was to get back to the church so I could get on with my *normal* ministry. Working with teens wasn't always sunshine and roses, but preaching and playing games was what I was called to do, right? Helping kids deal with family conflicts and self-esteem problems in the confines of my office was comfortable. *That* was what pastors did, I told myself. Visiting murderers in jail ... I'd leave that to the Gideons, to missionaries, or to bold new believers who'd been redeemed from lives of crime themselves. People like me ... well, I was called to disciple believers; you know, the ones who came into my office.

That's how I justified only going back to see Ronnie one more time in almost a decade. I imagine it's how a lot of us justify our lack of interaction with those who are locked up. But then, of course, we encounter this bothersome story that Jesus told his disciples when they asked Him about the end of this current age:

> *When the Son of Man comes in his glory, and all the angels with him, he will sit on his throne in heavenly glory. All the nations will be gathered before him, and he will separate the people one from another as a shepherd separates the sheep from the goats. He will put the sheep on his right and the goats on his left.*
>
> *Then the King will say to those on His right, "Come, you who are blessed by my Father; take your inheritance, the kingdom prepared for you since the creation of the world. For I was hungry and you gave me something to eat, I was thirsty and you gave me something to drink, I was a stranger and you invited me in, I needed clothes and you clothed me, I was sick and you looked after me, I was in prison and you came to visit me." Then the righteous will answer him, "Lord, when did we see you hungry and feed you, or thirsty and give you something to drink? When did we see you a stranger and invite you in, or needing clothes and clothe you? When did we see you sick or in prison and go to visit you?" The King will reply, "I tell you the truth, whatever you did for the least of these brothers of mine, you did for me."*
>
> *Then he will say to those on his left, "depart from me, you who are cursed, into the eternal fire prepared for the devil and his angels. For I was hungry and you gave me nothing to eat, I was thirsty and you gave me nothing to drink, I was a stranger and you did not invite me in, I needed clothes and you did not clothe me, I was sick and in prison and you did not look after*

me." They also will answer, "Lord, when did we see you hungry or thirsty or a stranger or needing clothes or sick or in prison, and did not help you?" He will reply, "I tell you the truth, whatever you did not do for the least of these, you did not do for me." Then they will go away to eternal punishment, but the righteous to eternal life (Matthew 25:31-46).

Well, that story stinks! What about my trip to the altar? What about my faith? What about all those days I got up early and went to church? Let us not misunderstand our Lord here: as the apostle Paul would later clarify (Ephesians 2:8-9), we are saved by grace through faith, not by works. There is no getting around that. But I am reminded that Jesus once clarified for his listeners how they could recognize false prophets:[2] by their fruit you'll recognize them, He said. In other words, *not everyone who says to me, 'Lord, Lord,' will enter the kingdom of heaven, but only he who does the will of my Father who is in heaven.* But Lord, they'll plead: didn't we prophesy in your name? Didn't we volunteer in your name? Didn't we preach, serve on church boards, give money?! Then I will tell them plainly, "*I never knew you. Away from me, you evil-doers!*"

Apparently, there will be many on that day who cry out His name. There will be many who say, "Wait! I called you my *Lord!*" Yet, Jesus makes clear the criteria by which He will distinguish the fakers from the followers. Again, this is not a theology of works. This has nothing to do with *earning* the inheritance of God. He is simply offering an illustration of how we'll know who loves Him. What marks the real sheep? The answer, it seems, is that *to follow Jesus is to care for the broken.* In order to more fully understand the breadth of this statement, I want us to explore together why it matters to God, why many of us normally don't do it, and what it looks like to be the true heirs of our King.

God is on the Side of the Weak

About five years ago, I decided to join the volunteer fire department in my community. Given that the time required to perform my pastoral duties at that point was not overwhelming me, I was looking for something else to do, some way to serve outside the walls of our building. Right about that time, a couple in our church began to talk up the merits of firefighting, eventually convincing me

---

[2] See Matthew 7:15-23.

to apply at the station down the street. When I agreed, I had all sorts of spiritual-sounding reasons I could list about wanting to help out, wanting to get to know people in my town.[3] But, do you want to know the truth? The biggest reason I said yes was simply that I'm a guy and I thought it would be awesome to fight fires. It was an adventure I had desired since childhood, and here was the perfect opportunity. So once I got voted onto the department, I started attending the regular weekly meetings: a training session, a business meeting, or some sort of work night. The first night, when I showed up and met a number of the guys, I learned two things really quickly: I do not fit in here, and I do not fit in here *at all*.

These guys told jokes I hadn't heard since high school (of the locker room variety). These guys used language most people try to hide from me because I'm the preacher. At least half of them had an impressive Hulk Hogan mustache, whereas it takes me 4 full weeks before anyone notices that I haven't shaved. When *they* show up for work night, they come in the clothes in which they actually *do work* throughout the week; but I spend most of my day in an office. Before *my* first meeting, I spent a half hour in my closet trying to find something to wear, thinking to myself, "Hmm, I guess I could get this a little *smudgy*." It was just a different world I was entering. At first, a couple of them had graciously reached out to me, and it was all progressing slowly along. Until ladder training night.

On ladder training night, we were all brought out to the front of the fire station. We put on our gear and were given the following instructions: get a ladder off the truck. Put it up to the roof. The first guy goes up and ties off the hose. The second guy goes up and brings the axe. Then the guy who's on the bottom will carry down the fireman who went up first. Then the other guy goes back up and brings down the equipment. Grab a partner and let's go. Meanwhile, my eyes are getting bigger by the second, and I'm still trying to figure out which one's the axe. So these guys started picking partners – you know, from the guys they actually trust – and lined up to take a turn. Predictably un-chosen, I just stood around and watched.

Before long, the assistant chief walked over towards me, and asked, "Ryan, have you gone yet?" But before I could answer, a man named Tracy answered for me: "He's going with me."

---

[3] You know, *connecting* with people, as we church folk are fond of saying.

Tracy was one of the few guys who had reached out to me early on. He found me the first night and offered to help any way he could, volunteering to meet me at the fire house to show me the trucks, answer questions, anything I needed. Tracy is probably one of the most respected men on the department, he has served in combat with the Army, and he's among the first on the truck every time we get a call; he truly knows his stuff. He's also about 235 pounds of *solid*, and everyone loves the guy. And in that moment, he walked over, in front of everyone, and declared, "He's going with me."

Both shocked and nervous, I didn't know what to say. Here's what I came up with, in a voice that slightly cracked: "You want me to go first or second?" And without hesitation, he responded, "You're going to carry me down." Meanwhile, everyone who was standing around just sort of went silent, as if to ask, "You're putting your life in the hands of Captain Clean Jeans? Seriously?" Even I was standing there, thinking, "you sure about this, big guy?" And Tracy, reading everyone's minds, looked me right in the eye and said, "I trust him."

So up the ladder we went. By the time I was nearly to the top, all the guys who had mostly ignored me up to this point were now beginning to shout up encouragements. And when it was time, the big man got into position, and I slowly walked him down the ladder.[4] My first instinct upon reaching the ground – after thanking the Lord that both of us were somehow still alive, of course – was to thank Tracy for what he'd done. He chose me when no one else would, and that gave me confidence amongst a group of people whom I'd found rather intimidating just moments before.

But the longer I've had to reflect on that day, the deeper my appreciation of Tracy has grown: he had literally put his life in my hands to prove a point; though ultimately, his willingness was not just meant for me. Here's what I mean: when I thanked him for choosing me, he said something that I've always clung to, personally. He said, "I believed in you. I knew you could do it." He may never

---

[4] Tracy and I would become great friends after that day. I've never told him, but I was completely terrified during that exercise. Had my hands, which were weakening with every step, slipped off the ladder, the two of us would have likely fallen to the ground, where his momentum (that's mass x velocity, kids) would have crushed me like a grape. In hindsight, I don't know if "I trust him" meant that he trusted me to get the job done, or if he simply trusted that my body would be sufficient to break our inevitable fall from the ladder.

know what that encouragement did for me, as a man. But what he said next was just as profound: "These men," he said, "needed to know they could trust you." Effectively, one of the most respected men on the department chose to align himself with the weakest member of the team, inviting others to do the same.

It is easy to assume that this passage in Matthew is about giving aid to the needy, and nothing more. To be sure, the sheep and the goats were separated on the basis of what they actually *did* for those who were suffering. But embedded within that narrative is a critical truth which we must not miss. Jesus said, whatever you did (or did not do) for the least of these, my brothers, you did (or didn't do) for me. He wasn't simply telling the listener that they should do good things for the poor and hurting; instead, He was *aligning Himself* with the weak, the disenfranchised, the broken, and the imprisoned, expecting His followers to do the same.

If you're a churchgoer, you've probably seen your fair share of Jesus emails. Some of them are wonderful illustrations of God's love. Others end with the warning that if you don't send this to 30 more people, little children will die and Jesus will hate you. Who knew He cared so much about email forwards?! But one I've seen a handful of times describes "Jesus in disguise." It takes a few different forms, but ultimately, the message is that sometimes Jesus visits us here on earth without us knowing. Usually, the visitor is a wise, older individual who shows us the true meaning of love or humility. It's a gracious person with a kind heart who offers us something tangible, even though he or she doesn't have much. He might be a simple man, but He's generally clean and safe.

Unfortunately, that's not necessarily the type Jesus identifies Himself with in this story, is it?[5] He doesn't exactly perpetuate the "Jesus in disguise" idea here, but clearly He connects Himself to a kind of person. Only, in His story, He's the dirty beggar on the street. He's the man who stops by the church asking for a handout, who seems half out of it. He's the woman whose body is rotting away in

---

[5] To be fair, the designation here in this passage has been disputed. While D. A. Carson concedes that "the great majority of scholars understand 'the least of these brothers of mine' (vv. 40, 45) to refer to all who are hungry, distressed, needy," he himself argues that the reference is limited to followers of Jesus. While he does make a solid case for his position, I have adopted the broader view, primarily based on the pattern of Christ Himself (as described in the next paragraph). For Carson's view, see Gaebelein, *The Expositor's Bible Commentary, Vol. 8*, pp. 519-520.

her own home. He's the guy who's stuck in jail, rarely seeing the light of day. He's not only the cute little kids you can send money to overseas! He's Ronnie in a jail cell, with a tear-stained face. Even the mere suggestion scandalizes some people, because *our* Jesus is clean! *Our* Jesus only identifies with the lowly of circumstance – not actual sinners![6]

But the Jesus of Scripture seemed to always be in and among the dirty. He was so identified with the poor, the sick, the sinners, that He was often accused of being one Himself! It was guilt by association. He touched the people that no one else would. He spoke to the people whom everyone else ignored. He ate dinner with the people whom everyone else was too clean to be around! And when the men who were entrenched in religion questioned His tactics, He said, the hookers and the cheaters are getting into the Kingdom before you. He surrounded Himself with the sick, the poor, the imprisoned and said, *these are my people.*

And then He turns the question on all who would hear this story and asks, are they your people too? Jesus identifies with the broken by becoming one of them. He says, whenever you helped (or *didn't* care) for one of these, you were doing it (or *not* doing it) for me. Yet, He doesn't call His followers to identify in quite the same way. He doesn't say, *become* sick, thirsty, naked, or imprisoned. Instead, He says that our identification with the broken is to actually do something.

James, the brother of Jesus, describes a scene that I think is all too common within the church when it comes to caring for the needy. He invites the reader to imagine that a person comes to you and has no clothes or food. Is it caring to simply say to them, "I wish you well"? To pat them on the back and say, "keep warm and well-fed"?! If you don't do anything, that faith you keep touting as your saving grace is actually dead and useless. Your concern for the sick, suffering and imprisoned is *active*, or it is nothing at all. Nevertheless, we still somehow find reasons to hesitate when it comes to such benevolence, don't we? Why do you suppose that is?

Why We Hesitate to Help

A very kind man came to our church not long ago with his elderly mother. They just needed a little gas money, he told me, as his mother was trying to get to a funeral for a family member. Her

---

[6] Please don't misunderstand: I am not at all suggesting that Christ Himself was sinful.

car was stranded up the road somewhere, but any help we could offer would be much appreciated. Happy to help, I took them down to the gas station on the corner and purchased a gift card to be used at any of their stations. Thanking me profusely, the two went about their way, leaving me to bask in the joy of having helped someone in need. That joy was short-lived, of course, when I heard a few days later that this pair had been going to churches all over town sharing the same fictitious story.

I have to admit that I was more than a little frustrated. Ours is not a wealthy congregation, and some are making a tremendous sacrifice to give what they do to the church. To discover that the resources entrusted to our care have been given to swindlers was disheartening, to say the least. Yet, this sort of thing happens to generous churches and individuals all the time; and unfortunately, a common response is to tighten our grip on what we possess. Sometimes, we opt to run those seeking assistance through a gauntlet of questions and paperwork to verify their need. Other times, we demand that they offer us something in return, like painting the church building or attending a service. Or, sometimes we just say no. After all, we don't want to be manipulated. At least that's what we tell ourselves, anyway.

I have a feeling, however, that the real reason we often choose not to extend care to the broken runs a bit deeper than that. Look again at the response of those deemed goats in verse 44: "Lord," they ask, incredulously, "when did we see you hungry or thirsty or a stranger or needing clothes or sick or in prison, and did not help you?" The implication, of course, is this: "Had we only known it was really you, we surely would have taken care of you!" Anyone who struggles with road rage can surely relate. When that jerk cuts you off, or just won't move out of the way fast enough, you're ready with either the prolonged horn-honk, the angry glare, or even the one-finger salute. But imagine if, no sooner do you express your displeasure than you come to realize that the recipient of your rage is your boss – or maybe even your pastor. I bet you would have considered a more measured response, had you only known who it was!

Similarly, when it comes to those who are broken, it's not that we aren't willing to help, we just want to know we're not being scammed; we want to know that the recipient is *deserving*! Again, we tell ourselves that's the problem. But one simple application likely reveals our own hypocrisy: *what if the person in need was your*

137

own child? If you saw your own son or daughter thirsting or hungering, would you provide food and water? Even if they had sinned against you, lied to you, schemed and rebelled in every way imaginable ... would you deny sustenance? What if your rebellious child was sick or imprisoned – would you go and visit? If your child was dying in a hospital or rotting away in a jail cell somewhere, would it really matter what they'd done or how they landed there? I guess I can't speak for you, but I have two children of my own, and I can tell you this: nothing on earth would stop me from getting to my kids and coming to their rescue if I saw them in need.

I have some people in my own family who would say the same thing. For years, their son took advantage of them. At different times, he found himself without resources, sick in a hospital, and ultimately even locked up in jail. Most of his troubles came as a direct result of poor and selfish decisions he had made; but every time, his parents sacrificed whatever was necessary to dig him out of his pit. They gave up thousands of dollars, they gave of their time – in fact, they missed so much work trying to help him out, that even their own jobs were put in jeopardy – and every time they did, it seemed to be wasted on frivolous purchases when he received the assistance.

What made it worse was that, in the midst of it all, rarely was there any sense of gratitude from their son. In his mind, it was as if they *owed* it to him, somehow. But even that wasn't enough; more than once, in spite of all they'd graciously given to him, he stole what little they had left. It got so bad at one point, that the rest of the family openly questioned his parents' wisdom. "You're just enabling him," they were told. "You're going to lose everything you have and end up with nothing," others said. They just didn't have the resources to be throwing money away. And to be perfectly honest, watching the pain they endured and the lack of change in their son, I began to foster my own frustration with them, casting judgment in my heart. How could they keep bailing him out like that?

But then one day, the Lord asked me a terribly penetrating question – one that completely transformed my assessment of this situation: In a quiet moment alone, He asked me, "Ryan, how much did I give up to rescue you?" *But God demonstrates his own love for us in this: While we were still sinners, Christ died for us.*[7] As I reflected on the magnitude of His mercy in my own life, I began to view my

---

[7] Romans 5:8.

family in a different light. Suddenly, I lost interest in judging whether or not that was the best possible parenting strategy,[8] or whether it was wise. Instead, I just found myself overwhelmed by an unrelenting love, which caused them to give everything they had for someone who continued to sin against them. They did it because he was their son, whether he manipulated them or not.

My point is this: we can tell ourselves that we refuse to help people because we don't want to be manipulated or to have someone take advantage of our kindness. But the truth is, most of us would help someone in need, even in spite of that, if we loved the person deeply enough. Thus, I would suggest to you that our biggest issue is not that we are too protective of our resources; rather, *the problem is that we do not love as Christ loves*. My guess is that the King will have no trouble believing that the goats would have offered assistance had they known it was Him. It's just that it doesn't really matter, because that's not the issue. For what it's worth, the sheep didn't know it was Jesus, either. They just extended mercy because, like their Master, they were on the side of the weak.

A Portrait of the True Heirs

It is in the light of this reality that we can safely reject any interpretation of Matthew 25 which suggests that somehow our acts of kindness to the poor will earn for us salvation. Again, those deemed to be goats *would have* done the service, under the "right" conditions. But it wasn't about that. No, those for whom the kingdom has been prepared are those who have been transformed in the image of the King Himself. Those who are commended for their faithfulness are those who love as He loves; they are those who identify with the poor and the broken, aligning themselves with the weak. For surely, that is who our Incarnate Lord was: "Down, down, says Christ; you will find Me in the poor; you are rising too high if you do not look for Me there."[9]

---

[8] Not that this necessarily answers the question, but for what it's worth, they currently have a wonderful relationship with their son. He ultimately found freedom from his addictions, does all he can to help and provide for them, and even recently began attending church. He is a different man today, and I can't help but think that their unconditional love played a significant role in the work God has been doing in him.
[9] From Martin Luther, as quoted by Matt Friedeman in his [*Evangelism*] lecture, *Compassionate Ministry, the Basics 2*, p. 2.

That said, we cannot ignore the implication that such a transformation will indeed produce fruit. That is, it is insufficient to speak of our *concern* for the poor and the neglected if it does not translate into active service (as we explored above). For the early Fathers of the church, such a merciful lifestyle was what set them apart from the world: "It is our care for the helpless, our practice of loving-kindness, that brands us in the eyes of many of our opponents," noted Tertullian.[10] To this, Chuck Colson has added the following:

> *The Bible requires...that we care about our neighbors, clothe the naked, feed the hungry, and visit the sick and those in prison. That's us the Lord is talking to, and we don't discharge that obligation by paying our taxes or dropping dimes in charity boxes. We discharge it by doing the Word of God.[11]*

His emphasis, it seems, is that it isn't enough to simply send money, that another might minister to the disenfranchised in your place. The expectation of all the true heirs of the King is that we would take an active role, wherever the Lord has seen fit to place us. Few followers of Jesus have embodied this conviction more clearly than the founder of Methodism, John Wesley. Even at the age of 82, he was known to trudge throughout the city – in ankle-deep snow, no less – seeking donations from those with means, that he might clothe the poor in his own neighborhood.[12] Personal involvement in this manner was both modeled and taught by Wesley. In His sermon, "On Visiting the Sick," he left the reader without excuse:

> *All therefore who desire to escape the everlasting fire and to inherit the everlasting kingdom are equally concerned...to practice this important duty. It is equally incumbent on young and old, rich and poor, men and women, according to their ability. None are so young, if they desire to save their own souls, as to be excused from assisting their neighbors. None are so poor (unless they want the necessaries of life) but they are*

---

[10] Ibid.

[11] As quoted by Friedeman, in his [*Evangelism*] lecture, *Compassionate Ministry and Cultural Evangelism: John Wesley*, p. 16.

[12] Friedeman, *Compassionate Ministry and Cultural Evangelism: John Wesley*, p. 10.

called to do something...for the relief and comfort of their afflicted.[13]

What excuses do you suppose we might offer to our Savior on that final day? What will we say to the one who set aside His glory to identify with the dirtiest wretches of humanity? Will we say that we were scared? Will we say that the sacrifice was too great? Will we say that we thought He'd called someone else to visit those who are imprisoned? I fear that if we do, we'll find ourselves parted off to the left. Dr. Matt Friedeman, a vibrant church-planter and Mississippi preacher, puts it a little more bluntly. He reminds us that on that day, Jesus will look to all those on the left and say, "You didn't feed me when I was hungry – *go to Hell*. You didn't clothe me when I was naked – *go to Hell*. You didn't visit me when I was sick, or when I was in prison – *go to Hell*."

On that day, there will be sheep and goats, and all of them may call Him Lord. Those who inherited the kingdom were those whose faith led them to actively identify with the broken. On which side will you be found?[14]

Practical Action Step

Perhaps I need not say much here, as the action step is somewhat obvious: go feed the hungry, visit the sick, clothe the naked, and visit the imprisoned. If you know someone in this situation, make it a priority this very week to minister in this manner. If you are at a loss as to whom you can offer such acts of mercy, fall to your knees this very moment and plead with the Lord to give you an opportunity. I have little doubt that He will answer your prayer, perhaps even today.

This serves as a practical action step, but we must not miss the deeper truth: our call is to love as He loves. We are to align ourselves with the weak. As you serve – not once, but habitually – ask that God would transform your heart, that you might learn to see the desperate as He sees them: as treasured children who are worth the sacrifice.

Still, some of us may be hung up on the potential for manipulation. "Am I really just to throw money at *anyone* who

---

[13] As quoted by Friedeman, *Compassionate Ministry, the Basics 2*, p. 5.
[14] As it happens, I have the opportunity before me to answer this question myself. By the grace of God, Ronnie recently wrote to me from prison, and we've since been corresponding to one another via letters.

asks?!" we wonder, horrified at the potential cost. Marvin Olasky frames a response to this question quite astutely. Regarding Wesley's admonition to deal with others as God would deal with us, Olasky adds, "The only question might be, how would we want God to deal with us? As a cold official who provides material without love? As a warm sugar daddy who gives without discipline?"[15] In the end, I expect that the Lord will provide us with all the discernment we need, if we are willing to trust Him in every encounter. So go and do it. In fact, as William Booth has reminded us:

> **You must do it**. With the light that is now broken in upon your mind and the call that is now sounding in your ears, and the beckoning hands that are now before your eyes, you have no alternative. To go down among the perishing crowds is your duty. Your happiness from now on will consist in sharing their misery, your ease in sharing their pain, your crown in helping them to bear their cross, and your heaven in going into the very jaws of hell to rescue them.[16]

[15]Olasky, M. (1992). *The Tragedy of American Compassion*. Washington: Regnery Publishing, p. 8.
[16] As quoted by Friedeman, *Compassionate Ministry, the Basics 2*, p. 5.

The Love of Money

"Two dollars on *David's Dandy* to show, please." I felt like such a little man. They took my money, I took their ticket – and, boy, did I have a good feeling about this.

For the first time in years, my Pappaw had come to town, and so our family celebrated by doing what he loved: going to the horse races. My grandfather lived in Florida, so I didn't ever get to see him very much; but when I did, I was absolutely delighted. He had a deep southern accent, which caused him to pronounce my name like no one else I knew. Coupled with his boisterous smoker's laugh, I just couldn't get enough of listening to him tell a story. I treasured the memories of lying next to him on the floor in front of his old television, watching the *Twilight Zone* together. And to top it off, I was reasonably certain that he was the strongest man I knew. Every day we were together, I would plead with him to flex his muscles, and every day, he'd hold out on me. I'd get to begging, he'd get to laughing, and then finally he would do it – albeit ever so briefly. He would hold up his arm, then flex for just a few seconds. And when he did, it was like a softball appeared out of nowhere under his skin. I was completely enthralled by my Pappaw, and so having him make the trip clear up to Ohio was a real treat for me.

Aside from sitting on a lawn chair in his garage and keeping an eye on his neighborhood, he had few real joys in life like watching horses careen around the track. And it just so happened that we had a track[1] within 45 minutes of our house. Though I'd lived near Columbus all my life, I'd never been to Scioto Downs before; but after that day I was sure I'd be back again.

---

[1] My Pappaw had my mom and her siblings at the track just about every weekend growing up, I'm told. He was into thoroughbred racing, but the track close to my home offered harness races. I imagine it was a step down for him, but it was better than nothing, I suppose.

At the start of the day, it was enough to watch my Pappaw get wound up about the horses he'd picked. He was having such a good time, yelling and laughing, that I was just content in his presence. But as a 10-yr-old kid, other people's joy only sustains you for so long – eventually, it sinks in that you're watching anonymous horses race around the same circle for hours. Yawn. Perhaps discerning my disinterest (and knowing that Pappaw was not nearly ready to go home), my parents decided to make it interesting for me. "Here's two dollars," Dad said. "Whenever you're ready, we can go down and place a bet on whichever horse you like."

My eyes must have lit up like it was Christmas. Now you're talking! Suddenly these anonymous horses racing around the same circle looked like dollar signs with hooves to me. My Pappaw handed me his racing guide, and I absolutely soaked it up. I had paid just enough attention to the grown-ups that day to know that I needed to pick a good horse, but not a great one. Those horses expected to win might be a wise choice for victory, but they weren't paying out much money. Meanwhile, those nags with a poor record might pay out a lot of money, but they likely had no shot. I needed a middle-of-the-pack animal. I needed a horse with just the right stats. I needed ... wait – is that one named *David's Dandy*?

His name jumped off the page like a flashing neon sign. As soon as I saw it, I had an epiphany: stats were significant, without question; but how was I supposed to sift through all the numbers? I was just a kid on my first day at the track. No, I needed a sure thing. I needed *the Lord* on my side. With merely two dollars in hand, God Himself was my only chance at becoming independently wealthy that day. And so, my logic went like this: King David was one of God's favorite guys. This horse has the name David. If I honor the Lord by picking a horse with the name of His favorite guy, He will surely reward my faithfulness (after all: if God isn't anxious to reward a 10-yr-old Bible-believing little gambler, whom *will* He bless?!). So, brimming with confidence,[2] I took my two dollars down to the window and cast my lot with *David's Dandy*.[3]

Once I made it back into the stands, I was a bundle of nerves. I mean, if ol' Dandy pulled off the upset, my whole life could change. I'd have to get a financial advisor. I'd probably eventually have to

---

[2] And by *confidence* I mean that I only picked him to come in third or better. He might have been the Lord's horse, but that was *my* [dad's] two dollars on the line.

[3] Who, as it happens, was also a horse with middling stats. Double bonus!

support my own parents. They were good eggs – I'd take care of them. But I was getting ahead of myself. First, the race.

And they're off! When the gates flew open, I closed my eyes. I just couldn't watch. All around me were the sounds of shouting people, thundering hooves, and incessant chatter from the announcer. I couldn't make out much of what he was saying, so after the first lap, I finally opened my eyes. Predictably, David's Dandy was in the middle of the pack. This would clearly prove to be no Secretariat-at-the-Belmont,[4] but we were still alive! Continuing down the back stretch, the horses began to sort themselves out, and the Dandy was in fifth. As I felt my riches beginning to slip away, I wondered where it all went wrong. Coming around the final turn, I resigned myself to the fact that my station in life would remain unchanged.

When suddenly, as if spurred along by angel's wings, David's Dandy surged forward. Passing up his opponent, he slid into fourth. Could it be? Did I have a shot? Pushing ahead with all his might, he passed another horse and was now in third. By this time I was standing and screaming, willing him forward with dollar signs in my eyes. By the time he crossed the finish line, he'd lunged past another poor sap and ended up in second place. *Second place!* As my family attempted to pat me on the back, they ended up swatting at the air, because I was already off to the ticket window to collect my winnings. In my mind, they'd just dump dollar bills into my outstretched arms ... maybe even put a crown on my head to pay homage to my sheer awesomeness. I'd do my best to handle the adulation with grace.

When I got to the window, I anxiously passed in my ticket and held out my hands. Quite unceremoniously, the disinterested person on the other side handed me my prize: nine dollars. Nine dollars? *Nine dollars!* I'm not sure my feet touched the ground all the way back to the stands. The only thing that even came close to deflating my celebration was the knowledge that I could have made at least five more dollars had I been bold enough to pick him to *place* (come in second). No matter. I'd [approximately] quadrupled my investment! Unfamiliar with any sort of increasing investment principles – and too cheap to ever risk more than $2 anyway – I quickly did the rudimentary math: if I placed these bets even just a quarter of a million more times, I'd be set for life!

---

[4] If, like me, you're young enough to have not seen this live, check out the race here: http://www.youtube.com/watch?v=xoFquax2F-k. Astounding.

Sadly, many of my memories from that day have faded. I don't remember how long we were there, or how many races we watched. I don't remember anything my Pappaw, who has since passed away, said to me during that outing. But as clearly as though it happened yesterday, I remember the thrill of winning that money, meager as it was.

Growing up, I never struggled with the particular temptations of drugs or alcohol. My parents didn't really need to worry that I would get hooked on a substance of any sort. But after that day, I was always keenly aware that if I ever started gambling, I'd have a hard time stopping. I recently heard John Piper say that he always donates the honorariums he receives for preaching all over the country. The reason, he said, is that he's afraid of what that kind of money would do to him. How true.

As a nation, we are crazy about money, aren't we? We celebrate monetary gain by making it effectively synonymous with the word *success*. We stand in awe of and highly acclaim those who have amassed fortunes which neither they (nor their children) could possibly spend in one lifetime. What's more, many of us are willing to do almost anything to get ahold of it. Most readers will be familiar with the name Bernie Madoff, who was sentenced in 2009 to 150 years in prison and called upon to forfeit nearly 18 billion dollars, which he gained by defrauding thousands of people who had invested with his financial firm. Think about that. In the pursuit of more money than he could ever spend, he was willing to rob thousands of all they'd worked so hard to save.

Others, of course, have gone even further. When I was a teenager, I remember hearing about a young person who had been gunned down simply so that the perpetrator could have the victim's high-priced shoes. *A person's life for a pair of shoes.* We hear stories like that, and we are probably all horrified. *I'd never dream of stealing or killing just to get money*, we tell ourselves. But my guess is that many of us are not altogether innocent on this count. Maybe it was a slight "adjustment" to our income figures on a tax return. Maybe we kept our thumb on top of the expiration date when we handed in that coupon. Maybe we lied about our child's age to get her into the amusement park for a cheaper rate. For anywhere from a few cents to a few dollars, some of us are willing to speak the very language of the devil (John 8:44), and we don't think much about it.

What is it about money that seduces us so? Honestly, I don't think the answer is too complex. In fact, my older sister taught it to me when we were young. As kids, whenever she and I would acquire some candy – on Easter, for instance – she always came into my room with a sweetness in her voice and a deal which seemed reasonable to a trusting child like me: "Ryan, how about we share your candy now, and we'll share mine later?" It's hard to say how many times I fell for that little gem. More times than I'd like to admit. So we would share my candy until it was gone; then, mysteriously, when I went to share her candy with her, she always claimed to be fresh out. Nevertheless, she somehow was eating candy all year. While her methods may have been suspect, her logic was sound: if I can store up enough for myself, my provisions will take care of me for quite some time. Likewise, I would suggest that we are so enticed by the acquisition of money for the very same reason. We believe that if we can take possession of enough money, *our stash* will provide for us and sustain us through the unforeseen tragedies of this life.

The problem, of course, is that this role belongs to Another.

As a pastor, if you want to see a dramatic increase in next Sunday's attendance, tell the people you're going to talk about sex. If, for some reason, you want to see the opposite trend, inform them that you'll be preaching about money. In far too many local churches, we have become convinced that the topic of money is off-limits. Preachers are afraid to talk about it, and congregants don't want to hear about it. Why? *Because how much I make and what I do with it is none of your business.* Somehow that area of our lives has come to be regarded as more personal than anything else we think or do.

Of course, Jesus didn't buy into that at all. Nelson Searcy argues that "Jesus was never afraid to talk about money ... in fact, if we were to teach about money as much as Jesus did, we would have to make it our topic every third Sunday."[5] Other than the Kingdom, he adds, money and possessions were His favorite thing to talk about – a topic which Jesus addressed more often than Heaven, Hell, faith and prayer. Why? "Because Jesus knew that this issue of money and possessions has the power to consume and derail us more quickly than anything else ... a fundamental connection exists between a person's spiritual life and his attitude toward money and possessions."[6]

---

[5] Searcy, N. (2010). *Maximize: How to Develop Extravagant Givers in Your Church.* Grand Rapids, MI: Baker Books, loc. 171 (Kindle Edition).
[6] Ibid.

Our Lord was well aware of the incredible power that money can have over us, and so He often drove a stake straight into the heart of the matter. And when He did, His message was clear: *to follow me is to reject the mastery of money in your life.* As we examine but one snapshot of His broad admonition on this subject, my hope is that we'll come away with, first, a more thorough understanding of the danger of loving money. This will, secondly, lead us into an exploration of more practical advice on how we ought to view and manage that which has been placed in our care.

The Danger of Possessions

> *"Do not store up for yourselves treasures on earth, where moth and rust destroy, and where thieves break in and steal. But store up for yourselves treasures in heaven, where moth and rust do not destroy, and where thieves do not break in and steal" (Matthew 6:19-20).*

Quick: what's your most prized possession? Whenever I consider that question, I often think of my basketball, which was signed by the 1999-2000 Los Angeles Lakers. While that team may not be of great significance to some, I bled and cried for that group of basketball players. This was, for those who do not know – or care – the team that secured Shaquille O'Neal's first championship ring. Outside of his own mother, I may be Shaq's biggest fan. And even though I came upon this little treasure by a bit of a fluke, it has always been tremendously meaningful to me.

Nevertheless, I didn't personally do anything to earn it. And as much as I enjoy having it, if it were gone tomorrow, I probably wouldn't miss it *that* much, as it merely sits underneath a glass case in my house. My real treasure is significantly less glamorous, but far more personal. Deep in the depths of my dresser drawer (second from the top) rests a gray t-shirt with these words printed in blue on the chest: *basketball champs.* For two straight years, as a young teenager, I signed up with my youth group to take part in a basketball tournament hosted by my denomination. And for two straight years, my team and I were humiliated by the competition. I was not much of a basketball player, but I loved to do it. And despite the fact that it was just a meaningless, one-day tournament in a church somewhere, it meant the world to me. Thankfully, on my third try, with a new batch of teammates, my friends and I achieved greatness.[7] We were sent home with a trophy, unhealthy pride, and these fabulous t-shirts.

Since this victory was achieved nearly 20 years ago, it is perhaps unnecessary to report that my championship t-shirt has seen better days. It has at least one rust stain, no sleeves, is nearly see-through, and smells like the inside of a shoe. One day, when I proudly will it to my son, there may be nothing left. Thus is the nature of our worldly goods.

Jesus began His statement with a clear *command:* stop storing up for yourselves treasures of this variety. Whether your passion is clothing, cars, collectibles, or cash, all of it could lay in ruin tomorrow. This very night, a thief could come along and take what you've worked so hard to acquire. By morning, the stock market could crash, and your life savings could be gone. But as He so ably points out, this is not true of treasure in heaven. Unlike all our wealth of goods here on earth, no one can take it, nothing can destroy it. Such treasure lasts forever in the heavenly realm. In this sense, then, the command is both positive and negative: *stop* doing what you're doing, and *start* doing something different. Stop chasing and collecting the wealth of the world, and start amassing the treasures of purity, faith, obedience, and love.[8] Effectively, Jesus is calling His listeners to establish new priorities.

Such a command, however, begs the question, *why?* After all, what's wrong with living comfortably? Isn't it responsible to see to it that my kids don't have to worry about their future? Sure, I could lose everything, but it's not like such a fate is common. It's not like the children of God *have* to be poor, right? Abraham was a man of incredible wealth. King Solomon had more riches and honor than any other person in all of his lifetime! What's the problem with a Christian who is amassing a fortune?

---

[7] Defining "greatness": In the interest of full-disclosure, we were technically all freshman (and sophomores) playing in what was supposed to be a junior-high league. It was allowed, though, because the upper age limit for that bracket was 15, which all of us were. At one point, one of my teammates nearly dunked on a 6th grader. I'd like to say I feel a little bad about winning in this manner ... but I don't. I have a shirt that says "Champs"!

[8] "The words 'treasures in heaven' go back to Jewish literature ... here it refers to whatever is of good and eternal significance that comes out of what is done on earth." See Gaebelein, *The Expositor's Bible Commentary, Vol. 8*, p. 177.

It would be tempting to suggest that Jesus has revealed the answer to this question already: that we must not store up such treasures, simply because they're fleeting. But I would argue that what He has said so far is merely a *description* of such treasures.[9] That is, while it is possible (even likely) that the contrast between the perishable treasures of earth and the imperishable treasures of heaven stands *in support* of the *why*, He has not actually revealed the answer in full. That comes in verse 21:

"For where your treasure is, there your heart will be also."

Thus, the problem is not merely that earthly treasures are not worth your devotion; *the problem is that your heart is attached to them.* "He is not saying that the heart should or should not be where the treasure is. He is stating the plain fact that wherever you find the treasure, you *will* find the heart."[10] Let me give you an example: when I was in college, my brother-in-law gave me a set of earth-shaking speakers for my car. I never had the money for such a thing at that point in my life, but I had always desired them. I was certain that if the ladies saw me cruising by in my 1987 white Honda, with enough bass to make your heart jiggle inside your chest, there would be a line of them waiting to claim me as their boyfriend. And although that scenario never materialized, I was thrilled about my speakers nonetheless.

Before long – as one might expect – I had trouble with my car stereo system. Knowing nothing about how to fix such things, I left my car in the capable hands of a family member while I went off to witness my first NBA game. Upon my return, I pulled up to the house, parking directly behind my Honda. As I did, I noticed a small light emanating from the edge of my trunk. Intrigued, I hopped out to investigate, only to find that my trunk was actually open. Of course, my precious speakers were nowhere to be found!

As you might imagine, I was horrified. Having your property stolen feels like an incredible violation anyway, but these speakers were the object of my desire and pride. I couldn't relax that night. I was angry, sad, and frustrated, to say the least. Though I eventually got over it, I was bothered for weeks. Ultimately, I had to ask myself

---

[9] Specifically, He does not command us to store up or not store up *because* these treasures can or cannot be destroyed. Instead, His comments simply provide contrasting descriptions of these types of treasures.
[10] Foster, p. 83.

this (and I would invite you to do the same): *when is the last time you were angry, sad, frustrated, and bothered for weeks over the fact that your neighbor is headed for Hell?* When is the last time you could barely relax or even sleep at night because you saw a homeless man wandering the streets? Do we care more about speakers or people?

As Matthew Henry has commented, "where the treasure is there the value and esteem are, there the love and affection are. Where the treasure is there our hope and trust are; there our joys and delights will be; and there our thoughts. The heart is God's due and that he may have it, our treasure must be laid up with him."[11] Put another way, our heart is the sum total of our will, affection, and desire; these belong to God, and the problem with attaching ourselves to worldly things is that we are devoting ourselves to something other than the Lord and His will.

Jesus continued, revealing not only the problem, but also the *effect* on us:

> *"The eye is the lamp of the body. If your eyes are good, your whole body will be full of light. But if your eyes are bad, your whole body will be full of darkness. If then the light within you is darkness, how great is that darkness!" (vv. 22-23).*

The connection between this section and the last is suggested by Proverbs 28:22 (KJV), which reads, "He that hasteth to be rich hath an evil eye."[12] If the problem is a divided heart (or here, an *evil/bad eye*), the effect on the person is a life filled with darkness. When our eyes are not singularly devoted to the Lord, we lack clear vision. What's more, we find ourselves separated from the life-giving presence of God.[13] This is why Jesus can so adamantly exclaim, "if then the light within you is darkness, how great is that darkness!" How desperate and poor we find ourselves – despite our net worth – when we separate ourselves from the light of God. Again, this impacts not only our vision and our priorities, but every aspect of our lives ("your *whole body* will be full of darkness").

---

[11] Church, p. 1231.

[12] See Carter, p. 38.

[13] Consider 1 John 1:5-6: "God is light; in him there is no darkness at all. If we claim to have fellowship with him yet walk in the darkness, we lie and do not live by the truth."

So He's given the command, He's told us why, and He's even revealed the effect on us. He closes, then, with a summary, getting right down to the *point* of it all:

"No one can serve two masters. Either he will hate the one and love the other, or he will be devoted to the one and despise the other. You cannot serve God and Money" (v. 24).

Finally, here, He paints a picture which reveals the heart of the matter, and the portrait is one of *mastery*. To live as a Christian is to submit to the Lordship of Christ. That is, because of His infinite, matchless love for me, I joyfully serve Him and invite Him to be the Master of my thoughts, my affections, my attitudes, my actions, and anything else He reveals to me. And yet, always vying for my allegiance, posing as a rival master to God, is the wealth of this world.

Make no mistake about it: you and I will pledge our allegiance to someone or something in this life. Whether we would admit as much or not, our lives reflect that we do choose a master. It may be God, it may be Money, it may be self, it may be any number of other people or things; but all of us choose something by which (or by whom) we make our decisions and plot our course. The point that Jesus here makes is that you cannot simultaneously devote yourself to two masters. When push comes to shove, one of them is relegated to second place, thus betraying the truth: *that* one wasn't really our master all along.

So who, or what, is your master? In the end, as I said at the beginning, it is all about *trust and dependency*. We are willing to serve that master whom we believe will most adequately care for us. So who or what will you trust to provide for you? Who or what do you really believe has the capability to sustain you through the trials of life?

I bet you're thinking of an answer right now.

I wonder if it's the same answer that is supported by the evidence of your life.

Perhaps it would help us to reflect on this more honestly if we consider a common example. Let's imagine that you and your family own two vehicles,[14] one of which is used sparingly. It's not

---

[14] The average family in America is said to own 2.28 vehicles. Interestingly, when comparing 1-car households, 2-car households, and those with three or more vehicles, the largest percentage of families is in the latter category

that two of you never need to be in separate places at the same time, but let's just say it's not a daily need. One day, you find out that a single mom in your church just totaled her car, on her way home from running errands. She's got two kids, each with rigorous sports schedules, and she has no means to purchase something else. She is unable to get a car loan, and couldn't pay one off if she could. What's more, she doesn't live near family, and they don't have the ability to assist in this manner anyway. The way you hear about it is on a Sunday, when the pastor stands and invites the congregation to pray that God would somehow provide for her a vehicle. As you bow your head to pray, these words enter your mind, seemingly out of nowhere: *give her yours*.

Would you do it?

Whoa! Hold on there! What about once a week when my spouse and I both need a vehicle? What would we do then? What about all the money I spent on that car? What if our other car broke down and we didn't have a back-up? If we give away our security blanket, how can we be sure someone will be there to take care of us if we find ourselves in the same predicament she's in?

I imagine our thought-process might look something like that. And by our very questioning, we shed light on the reality of our trusted source of provision. Does my spare vehicle keep me secure? Does what I've worked for and "earned" keep me from being in need (or simply inconvenienced)? *Or do we really trust in the Father who has promised to provide all that we need?*

I get that this is uncomfortable. I am not suggesting that we are free to be frivolous, poor stewards of our resources, or idle while others work – the Scripture directly refutes that approach to life (e.g., see 2 Thessalonians 3:6-15). I'm not even arguing that God is not your Master if you don't give away your car right now. But I am reminded that when the rich young man asked Jesus what He needed to do to inherit eternal life, Jesus responded, "One thing you lack. Go, sell everything you have and give to the poor, and you will have treasure in heaven. Then come, follow me."[15]

The insidious deception to which many of us have fallen victim is that it is sufficient to *say* that Money is not our master, even while the pattern of our lives reflects otherwise. Or as Foster puts it,

---

(34, 31, and 35 percent, respectively). See
http://www.autospies.com/news/Study-Finds-Americans-Own-2-28-Vehicles-Per-Household-26437/.
[15] Mark 10:21.

"we deceive ourselves if we believe we can possess the inward reality without it's having a profound effect on how we live."[16] Jesus didn't ask the man if he *would be willing* to give up his treasure on earth. My guess is that he, like many of us, would have said yes. Instead, Jesus told him to *go and do it*. It was through obedience to this that the man could have been faithful to the command to store up treasure in heaven. Instead, he went away sad, clinging to his true master. So, again, who is your master?

Leaving the Service of Money

I know it's a little late in the game to be confessing this, but I'm terribly uncomfortable writing this chapter; I can only imagine what it is like to be reading it. Maybe you've put it down already, out of sheer frustration. Maybe you just respectfully disagree.[17] Or, maybe you are wrestling under the weight of genuine conviction. Maybe you are coming to the realization that your faith and security have been found not in God, but in the possessions and resources you've acquired for yourself. If that is you, how do you break free and invite God to be the trusted and beloved master of your heart?

Over two hundred years ago, John Wesley wrote a painfully insightful sermon entitled *The Use of Money*. In it, he offers three plain rules by which the Christian can become a faithful steward of money. I have found Wesley's three rules to be remarkably simple to comprehend but more than challenging to practice; as such, I contend that they still today can serve us well as a trustworthy guide. It is important first to be reminded, however, of the principle with which he begins: "'The love of money,' we know, 'is the root of all evil;' but not the thing itself. The fault does not lie in the money, but in them that use it."[18] Let us not forget this: there is nothing wrong with money. There is nothing wrong with a Christian who earns a considerable amount of it. Furthermore, it is not only the wealthy who are plagued by the love of money – the pursuit of worldly treasure is not simply a matter of whether or not you've been successful in doing so. The problem, as I pointed out earlier, is that some of us have opted to place our trust in it (rather than our

---

[16] Foster, p. 79.

[17] If this is you, at least do yourself the favor of exploring *why* you disagree. At least be willing to ask yourself if your position on wealth is informed by the text of Scripture.

[18] Wesley, J., *Sermon 50: The Use of Money*. From *The Works of John Wesley, Vol. 6* (Reprinted in 2007). Grand Rapids, MI: Baker Books, p. 126.

heavenly Father), making it our master. Here, then, are Wesley's three rules to avoid such folly: *gain all you can, save all you can, and give all you can.*

First, *gain all you can.* Wesley is quick to qualify this, of course, noting that one must "gain all you can by honest industry."[19] That is, do not gain riches at the cost of human life or human suffering. Do not gain riches dishonestly, at the cost of your own integrity. Do not gain wealth if it means that your neighbor must be harmed in any way – this word "neighbor" includes, of course, your family. How many parents have pursued possessions and positions at such a tremendous cost of time that their children barely knew them? I once heard Andy Stanley say that someone else can and will do your job one day; but no one else can be your child's mom or dad. No one else can fill your role to your spouse.[20] So keep these caveats in mind; but under appropriate conditions, feel free to gain all you can.

Secondly, as you gain, be sure to *save all you can.* Lest we think he is promoting selfish hoarding, perhaps a more helpful way to clarify his emphasis is to say that we must not be wasteful. That is, rather than encouraging us to store away every last bit, he is advising the reader to *live simply.* Here I find Foster's work[21] to be of tremendous value. Commenting on the outward expression of simplicity, he urges the reader to purchase products for their usefulness, rather than status; reject anything that you notice is producing an addiction in you. Don't get sucked in, he writes, by the constant pressure of a culture telling you that you have to have every new gadget under the sun (iPhone 19, anyone?), or by the immediate gratification of "buy now, pay later." Or how about this: "Learn to enjoy things without owning them."[22] My favorite, though, is his suggestion to develop the habit of de-accumulation; that is, give things away, simply to break their hold on you![23] When is the last time you gave away something you really liked and regularly used, simply because someone else needed it? To return to Wesley, gain all you can, but don't buy all you can.

---

[19] Ibid., p. 130.

[20] I'm paraphrasing a bit. I believe what he actually said was, "No one else can be my wife's *first* husband." You get the point.

[21] See Foster, pp. 90-93.

[22] Foster, p. 93.

[23] And I assume he means more than simply the old, nasty clothes you refuse to wear anyway.

Finally, *give all you can.* He reminds the reader that we are but stewards of God's possessions. They are in our hands not simply for our selfish *enjoyment* (or "blessing," as we might say, to put a Christian stamp on our greed); rather, they are given to us that we might be faithful in doing His work. So first, provide what you *need* for you and your household. After that, take care of your brothers and sisters in Christ. After that, take care of all those in need. In this manner, "render unto God, not a tenth, not a third, not half, but all that is God's, be it more or less; by employing on yourself, your household, the household of faith, and all mankind, in such a manner that you may give a good account of your stewardship ..."[24]

Gain all you can, save all you can, and give all you can. It's fabulous advice. But perhaps our best practical wisdom comes from Jesus Himself, in the verses which follow the text which we've been exploring thus far:

> *Therefore I tell you, **do not worry about your life**, what you will eat or drink; or about your body, what you will wear. Is not life more important than food, and the body more important than clothes? Look at the birds of the air; they do not sow or reap or store away in barns, and yet your heavenly Father feeds them. Are you not much more valuable than they? Who of you by worrying can add a single hour to his life? And why do you worry about clothes? See how the lilies of the field grow. They do not labor or spin. Yet I tell you that not even Solomon in all his splendor was dressed like one of these. If that is how God clothes the grass of the field, which is here today and tomorrow is thrown into the fire, will he not much more clothe you, O you of little faith? So do not worry, saying, "What shall we eat?" or "What shall we drink?" or "What shall we wear?" For the pagans run after all these things, and your heavenly Father knows that you need them. But **seek first his kingdom and his righteousness**, and all these things will be given to you as well. Therefore do not worry about tomorrow,*

---

[24] Wesley, p. 135. While we're here, in this section (p. 134) Wesley also offers these questions (slightly paraphrased) as filters we ought to use before we spend money on non-necessities: 1) Am I here acting as a steward of God's goods? 2) Am I doing this in obedience to His word? Which verse? 3) Can I offer up this expense as a sacrifice through Christ? 4) Have I reason to believe that this expense will result in an eternal reward at the resurrection? Ask those next time you're at the store, I dare you.

*for tomorrow will worry about itself. Each day has enough
trouble of its own (Matthew 6:25-34, **emphases mine**).*

What better advice could there be to wrap this up? First,
choose not to worry about how your needs will be met. Your Father
loves you more than you could possibly know, and He knows exactly
what you need. If He takes such great care of common flowers in the
field, He'll take care of you. And secondly, once you are relieved of
worrying about your provision, you are free to set your concerns on
the kingdom and righteousness of God. Set your heart to the pursuit
of Him – His will and His nature – and you'll have all you need. *Do
you believe that?* Let the pattern of your life be your answer.

Practical Action Step
Ok, this one you may not like, but here goes: give something
significant away this week: not a bagful of old clothes, not the waffle-
maker you don't use anymore. I mean, give those away if you want,
but I'm talking about something you like. Don't just look around the
house and pick something you think you can comfortably live
without. Instead, ask the Lord to reveal to you a need. I know this is
scary, but ask Him to bring someone to your mind or along your path
this very week who needs something you have. Then, in the strength
and grace of God, choose to bless someone else with the provisions
God has placed in your care.

Perhaps this is a good time to be reminded that giving away
one item (alone) doesn't break the grip of Money's mastery over us.
Again, these practical action steps don't work that way. It's simply
meant to serve as the first – and sometimes most difficult – step
towards a new pattern of faith as we follow Jesus.

The Power Lunch

Though everyone around him was gripped with fear, the kid stood tall. Most of the men didn't know how the boy got there, or even who he was. Yet, they quickly realized that their fate was resting in his young hands.

For weeks now, they'd been in a standoff with the Philistine army, both sides restless in their respective camps. But day after day, both morning and evening, the scene in the valley played out in the same way: this monster of a warrior – Goliath, they'd heard was his name – would stand before the Israelite army and curse their God. He called the soldiers every insulting name that came to mind, pleading for just one man – any man – to come and fight. You see, the deal was simple: if Israel's best warrior could kill him, the Philistines would voluntarily become their slaves; but if Goliath proved victorious, Israel would have to submit to them.

In any other situation, it probably would have seemed like a reasonable arrangement. The problem, of course, was that no man in Israel could possibly win such a fight. No, seriously, it was *impossible*. Goliath was bigger than they thought a man could get. At over 9 feet tall, he was almost twice as big as many of the Israelites. He wore heavy body armor, the likes of which they'd never seen. Looking more like a machine than a man, he inspired such fear that the Israelites ran at the mere sound of his booming, threatening voice. For what it's worth, King Saul had offered incredible wealth, the hand of his daughter in marriage, and exemption from [ever] paying taxes to the man who would meet this giant in battle ... but he may as well have offered the moon. As near as all these soldiers could tell, a dead man wouldn't be able to benefit from any of that.

For his part, David was actually just delivering bread and cheese when he stumbled into the narrative. Too young to serve in the army, he was relegated to shepherding in the fields. He was merely checking on his older brothers when Goliath came out to insult and challenge the Israelites once again. But unlike the men all around him, David's reaction was not one of terror; instead, he found himself in disbelief: *"Who is this uncircumcised Philistine that he should defy the armies of the living God?"*[1] Despite his brothers' best efforts to silence him, David made his way around the camp, asking others the same question. Before long, the King himself stepped in, calling the kid into his tent.

For David, the challenge of the giant was no challenge at all: "I've fought all sorts of big, dumb animals," he told the King. "The Lord delivered me all those times – surely He will do it again. There's no reason for everyone to lose heart over all this! I'll go fight the big guy." It's hard to say why Saul finally consented; and yet, ultimately he did. But if David was going to go and give his life for the sake of Israel, Saul wasn't going to let him go alone: "Um ... here, at least wear my armor." How very noble. But, as David tried it out in the tent, he looked about like you'd expect a kid to look in a king's battle armor – ridiculous.

So David graciously declined, taking it all off. *"I cannot go in these,"* he said to Saul, *"because I am not used to them."*[2] David wasn't a soldier, he was a shepherd. And so he took the tools of a shepherd: a staff in one hand, a sling in the other, and five stones from the stream dropped into his shepherd's bag. It was hardly an intimidating armory, but that's what he knew. And with those rudimentary items, David stepped into the valley and changed the course of history. *In the name of the Lord Almighty, he did the impossible.*

If you ask my 9-yr-old son, *David and Goliath* is the best story in all of Scripture. The same could likely be said for many children. With nothing but a sling shot and a river rock, a *kid* takes down one of the world's most fearsome warriors! He beat a *giant*, after all! My son loves this episode, primarily because it makes him feel empowered. That is, if a shepherd boy can conquer a giant, maybe so can he. In reading the account of another's heroism, he is reminded that perhaps he, too, can be a hero.

Ironically, as I have grown older and experienced more of life, I find that this story tends to have quite the opposite effect on

---

[1] 1 Samuel 17:26.
[2] 1 Samuel 17:39.

me. Whereas once I was inspired by David's boldness in the face of danger, I often now feel dwarfed by it. As a child, all I could see is what lay ahead of me: a future filled with possibilities. I could become anything I wanted to be, I was told! I, too, could be a hero in a desperate situation. I too could slay a giant, so to speak. But then I didn't. Instead, I was just ... me. I became a man with some abilities, sure, but simultaneously a man with a lot more limitations. Therefore, every story of heroism – be it in the Bible or in the news – became a something of a taunt: *that's something you could never do.* It was just a painful reminder of my own [relative] frailty.

Faced with a physical challenge, I suppose there's always hope. With enough adrenaline surging through our bodies in an actual emergency, who knows what we could accomplish?[3] When it comes to the spiritual life, however, many of us have a tendency to believe that we're largely bound by who we've been thus far. When we see others seemingly living free from addiction, free from bitterness, free from pain, and free from temptation, it only serves to highlight our own spiritual weaknesses. When we see other Christians taking bold leaps of faith in their careers or in their personal lives, we're only reminded of our own crippling fears. In other words, every example of a passionate follower of Christ becomes something of a taunt: *that's something you could never be.*

My hope is that, as you've worked your way through this book, you've discovered (or *re*discovered) the joy of actually following Jesus. In offering these practical steps of obedience, my desire is that you've been drawn closer to your Savior; and, as a result, that you have experienced His power and mercy in a truly meaningful way. This has certainly been my intent. And yet, perhaps you've read these chapters and only come away feeling smaller. It would be great to take a leap of faith, to truly forgive my enemies, to become a person of prayer, to serve the broken, to make disciples, and to give away some of my earthly treasures, but ... *I'm just me.* I'm weak. I don't have a ton of talents to offer, and I struggle just to make it to church on [most] Sundays.

If you've ever felt that way when it comes to Christian discipleship, this final chapter is written for you. You are not the

---

[3] With the stories we hear on the news, does it not seem like a *given* that every mom in America could lift a small car off her child if she had to? They say it's adrenaline. But I have to admit, when I'm huffing and sweating just trying to get the big bags of salt from my car to my water softener, I quietly wonder if adrenaline could really bridge that gap.

only follower of Jesus to have felt inadequate. You are not the only disciple to have wondered if you really can keep in step with the Son of God; we need only examine the Scripture for supporting evidence. And this particular piece of evidence is pretty special. In fact, the story we're about to explore together holds the distinction of being the only miracle mentioned in all four gospels. "This fact alone should alert us to its significance."[4]

> The apostles gathered around Jesus and reported to him all they had done and taught. Then, because so many people were coming and going that they did not even have a chance to eat, he said to them, "Come with me by yourselves to a quiet place and get some rest." So they went away by themselves in a boat to a solitary place. But many who saw them leaving recognized them and ran on foot from all the towns and got there ahead of them. When Jesus landed and saw a large crowd, he had compassion on them, because they were like sheep without a shepherd. So he began teaching them many things.
>
> By this time it was late in the day, so his disciples came to him. "This is a remote place," they said, "and it's already very late. Send the people away so they can go to the surrounding countryside and villages and buy themselves something to eat." But he answered, **"You give them something to eat."** They said to him, "That would take eight months of a man's wages! Are we to go and spend that much on bread and give it to them to eat?" "How many loaves do you have?" he asked. "Go and see." When they found out, they said, "Five – and two fish." Then Jesus directed them to have all the people sit down in groups on the green grass. So they sat down in groups of hundreds and fifties.
>
> Taking the five loaves and the two fish and looking up to heaven, he gave thanks and broke the loaves. Then he gave them to his disciples to set before the people. He also divided the two fish among them all. **They all ate and were satisfied**, and the disciples picked up twelve basketfuls of broken pieces

---

[4] Gaebelein, *The Expositor's Bible Commentary, Vol. 9*, p. 71.

of bread and fish. The number of the men who had eaten was five thousand. (Mark 6:30-44)

Faced with a considerable need amidst masses of people, Jesus gave His disciples a fascinating word of instruction: *you take care of it.* Chew on that for a moment. Even as I type these words, I can't help but laugh. *You give them something to eat?* That's ridiculous. *He's* Jesus! *He's* the miracle man! *They're* only human. What He asked of them seemed impossible. And yet, incredibly, "they all ate and were satisfied." How did that happen? How did they get from point A to point B? That is precisely what I expect we will discover in this passage, as we look at the *problem*, the *resources*, and the *solution*.

The Problem

During the spring of my junior year of high school, I was trying to line up a job for the summer. I didn't have in mind any particular field of work, but I did have two criteria guiding my search: I wanted 1) lots of money and 2) little required of me. That's not too much to ask, right? I had a sense that I would be much better off working for an individual than for a business in town, given that I could probably charm my way into a more flexible schedule, if I was only dealing with one person. Much to my delight, at some point that spring, a friend of my Mom's asked if I might be interested in working at his property for the summer. My buddy Franco had worked for him the previous summer and had spoken highly of the job. Mostly, he told me, it involved mowing the man's expansive lawn and taking care of some chores out in the barn. That didn't sound so bad! Count me in, I told him.

Ever the astute businessman, this gentleman invited me first to come out one Saturday before school let out to get a feel for the work. My first job, he told me, would be to prep the lawn for mowing. That seemed easy enough, I said. How do I do that? Oh, just go through and pick up any sticks that are bigger than your pinky, he told me. Where do you want me to do that? *All over*, he replied. As I surveyed the land, in hindsight, the portions to be mowed were probably no more than an acre. At the time, it seemed like miles. Trees were everywhere, and there had recently been a significant rainstorm. In other words, the odds of taking a step in his yard and *not* landing on a decent-sized stick were akin to winning the lottery. I quickly discovered that my first job that day would also

162

be my *only* job.[5] I picked up sticks for hours, and I didn't even get close to finishing the task. I was in a sea of sticks, it seemed, and it felt like my efforts weren't even making a dent.

I can only imagine how the disciples must have felt as they looked out into this sea of hungry people, desperate to be near the Messiah. Many were sick, some were troubled, and others were simply curious. Clearly, they had needs. But the truth was, this little trip was supposed to be a private getaway for the disciples. They had just returned from a period of intensely difficult ministry, where they had personally preached repentance, driven out demons and healed the sick. They were likely spiritually, physically, and emotionally drained – not to mention pretty hungry themselves. Jesus had invited them on a mini-retreat of sorts, to recoup and to be nourished.

But the locals had something else in mind. Somehow recognizing their group (and likely their reputation for healing), the people ran ahead of them to the other side of the Sea of Galilee. Carter emphasizes their desperation, suggesting that they likely traveled eight miles by foot, taking the long way around, in the hopes of being ministered to by Jesus.[6] What was once looking like a nice, peaceful day to recover from the spiritual warfare in which they'd been engaged, was now portending to be an overwhelming continuation of service. The sheer number of people must have been daunting. All four gospels report that the number of men who were present was five thousand, which does not include women and children. Some have thus suggested a total crowd size of fifteen to twenty thousand![7]

Needless to say, when they stepped off that boat, they encountered tremendous need. What I find particularly interesting is the contrast in response between Jesus and His disciples. Look again at verse 34: "When Jesus landed and saw a large crowd, he had compassion on them, because they were like sheep without a shepherd. So he began teaching them many things." When Jesus encountered the need, He was moved by compassion to action. He too had likely been anticipating the rest and recovery afforded by

---

[5] Similarly, my first day of work for this gentleman also turned out to be my only day of work for him. Whether or not he had intended, through this preview, to weed out the lazy applicants, that was indeed the result. I sought another position for the summer. I'm not proud.
[6] Carter, p. 152.
[7] Gaebelein, *The Expositor's Bible Commentary, Vol. 8*, p. 342.

some private time away; and yet, He saw the people and brought them to Himself.

In contrast, consider the reaction of the disciples later in the day (vv. 35-36): "By this time it was late in the day, so his disciples came to him. 'This is a remote place,' they said, 'and it's already very late. Send the people away so they can go to the surrounding countryside and villages and buy themselves something to eat.'" Like Jesus, they too observed the great need of this massive crowd; however, their response was markedly different. As it can be difficult to read motives into a narrative, I don't believe we are compelled to suggest that their request was not a compassionate one. It is possible that they just wanted some peace for themselves, but it is certainly just as feasible that they, too, were moved by concern for the people. Even if that is, in fact, the case, notice the critical difference in their response: whereas the compassion of Christ caused Him to draw them near to Himself, the disciples suggested (be it out of love, or not) that He *send them away*.

The question before them, I suppose, could be summarized thusly: *whose problem is this*? When unexpectedly confronted with a massive need, Jesus clearly embraced a responsibility to engage and help. When the disciples saw such a need, their immediate reaction was to call upon the Lord to release the people, that they might help themselves. At the very least, we could say that they expected Jesus to handle it ("send the people away"); but the Savior declined. Instead, He called upon them to follow His own example by taking responsibility: *You give them something to eat*. Was that even reasonable?

The Resources

One day, when I was in third grade, my teacher, Mrs. Cornwell, had reached her limit. I don't recall that our class had been *drastically* misbehaving, but I guess the perspective of a child and that of an adult weren't really compatible in this case. Whatever had been going on, she'd had enough. Certainly, she'd given us warnings that we needed to change our ways – even if she hadn't, her slowly reddening face should have tipped us off – but we blithely ignored them.

As we continued in our merriment, I still remember watching her approach the door to the classroom. Tall and thin though she was, she looked remarkably like a boiling teakettle in that moment before that squealing whistle breaks loose. When she reached the door, her face was red and her jaw was clenched, as she subtly rose to her tip-toes to fire off this instruction at the top of her lungs: "Every one of you, get out your social studies books and copy chapter 3 … in Japanese!" With that, she stormed out of the room.

I didn't know precisely what she was hoping to elicit with that outburst, but what she got was silence. I mean to tell you that we went from a raucous crowd of miscreants to stone-faced silence in the blink of an eye. We could only look at one another with eyes wide, as if to ask, "Do you know Japanese? Because I … I don't think I do." To be honest, I didn't know what to do. But, ever the dutiful student, I got out my social studies book and opened it to chapter 3. I had copied about a sentence – in English – before I stopped and thought to myself, "She'll probably figure out this isn't Japanese." None of us knew what to do, because the request was simply preposterous. As a result, many of us chose to do nothing.

Apparently, the Lord's instruction for them to provide food for upwards of 20,000 people was similarly mystifying. *Feed these people?!* they asked, incredulously. "That would take eight months of a man's wages! [Do you honestly expect us] to go and spend that much [money] on bread and give it to them to eat?" Quick question: do you suppose that between the twelve of them, they simply didn't *have* that much money, or they just couldn't believe they were being asked to *donate* it? I cannot say for sure. But when we take into consideration the late hour, their remote location, the quantity of bread needed, and the expense involved, this just wasn't happening.

Perhaps another way to look at it is that the disciples were paralyzed by what they *couldn't* accomplish. In their mind, this problem had but one solution, and they knew they were not equipped to make it happen. Yet, as it turns out, Jesus wasn't at all interested in what they couldn't do. Instead, He invited them to begin engaging in what they *could* do.

> *"How many loaves do you have?" he asked. "Go and see." When they found out, they said, "Five – and two fish." Then Jesus directed them to have all the people sit down in groups on the green grass. So they sat down in groups of hundreds and fifties (vv. 38-40).*

With two basic instructions, Jesus transformed their understanding of the seemingly insurmountable problem before them. Can you men adequately acquire enough bread to feed thousands of people? Not likely. But what you *can* do is assess and gather our resources. You *can* organize the people in groups, to more easily facilitate the distribution of food. So that is precisely what they did. And in so doing, they revealed to us what is perhaps the most fundamental truth of discipleship: *to follow Jesus is to willingly offer what you have.* When the Lord called upon His men to give the people something to eat, He wasn't making an impossible demand; He just wanted them to willingly offer the resources and capabilities at their disposal – nothing more, nothing less.

Interestingly, the disciples were not the only ones who offered what they had. In John's version of these events, the five loaves and two fish were provided by one boy.[8] Think about his sacrifice. Mom may have packed this meal for him to sustain him through the day, and yet now it was being asked of him to offer them up to the disciples. I suppose he could have hidden his food, when the search was made for supplies. He could have greedily gobbled them up, filling his own belly before the opportunity was lost.[9] After all, not even a child would have assumed that such a small meal could feed so many people. And yet, he gave what he had.[10]

It seems like a pathetic offering in the face of such a massive dilemma. For that matter, so does the disciples' contribution of searching for food and organizing the people into groups. Yet somehow, it was enough. The reason, of course, was that they were not the only ones offering up the resources they had at their disposal.

The Solution

Taking what the disciples – and the boy – offered Him, Jesus looked up to heaven, gave thanks, and began divvying up the food. Then, notice that He gave it to the *disciples* to pass out to the people (v. 41 – their *third* contribution). Miraculously, all the people ate and were satisfied. Read that again: one meal, fit to serve just one boy, sated the hunger of [potentially] fifteen to twenty thousand people. And when they had all eaten, the disciples collected twelve

---

[8] See John 6:9. Notably, both the loaves and the fish are described here as "small."

[9] This works great when someone wants to share your Reese's Pieces ... or so I've been told.

[10] Technically, it is unclear as to whether he *volunteered* his food, or if he was, to borrow a term from my military friends, volun-*told* that he would be providing dinner. Either way, he handed them over!

166

basketfuls of leftovers (v. 43 – their *fourth* contribution, if you are still keeping track).

It goes without saying that I don't know *how* He did it. I don't know what it looked like as five loaves and two tiny fish were somehow being divided 20,000 ways. I only know that it was enough. *In the hands of Jesus, what His followers brought to Him was enough.* In fact, as the twelve extra baskets testify, it was *more* than enough. Walter Wessel is quick to point out the obvious (albeit profound) reality: "there was more left over at the end than there had been at the beginning."[11]

In the end, it was Jesus Himself who performed the miracle. It was Jesus who offered the solution to the problem. But I think we make a careless interpretive error when we reduce this account to nothing more than a statement about the abilities of Jesus. Now please don't misunderstand: Jesus is and always will be the central focus of the Gospel narrative. What's more, His power is unquestionably the source of our hope – in this story as well as all others. With that said, the text makes it clear that our Lord is also teaching us something about ourselves.

Carter summarizes this lesson as well as anyone:

> **Give ye them to eat** *(v. 37). The Greek is even stronger: "you yourselves give them to eat" (same in all three Synoptics). The command seemed utterly unreasonable. But the important point is that the disciples actually did exactly the impossible thing Jesus told them to do: they fed the whole crowd. He furnished the miracle; they furnished the hands; and the deed was done. Christ's disciples still have only one responsibility – obedience. It is His responsibility to provide the enabling power, as He did back there.*[12]

Throughout the entire account, Jesus is not only concerned with performing a miracle; He is also intentional about calling for the participation of His followers. When faced with an overwhelming

---

[11] Gaebelein, (Vol. 8) p. 674. To this, Carson adds an interesting comment, positing that the twelve baskets may be significant in that they allude to the twelve tribes of Israel. Though he does not force such a connection, he maintains that "the best suggestion may be that Messiah's supply is so lavish that even the scraps of his provision are enough to supply the needs of Israel." Ibid., p. 342.

[12] Carter, p. 152.

need, He expected His disciples to follow the very example which He Himself had provided: care enough to offer whatever they had. I would suggest that His invitation likewise extends to you and me today. Our Lord is not calling for the spiritual elite to go out and boldly change the world. He wants the humble, the meek, the broken and the weak to join in His ministry to the world. He still wants His faithful to offer whatever it is we have, in the full anticipation that it will be more than enough in His powerful hands.

A Final Word

So what do you have to offer? Not long ago, my wife and I were discussing a financial need in our household, admittedly stressing a bit about the magnitude of what it would cost us. The total amount was significant for us, and we weren't quite sure how we were going to come up with the cash by the time we needed it. Unbeknownst to us, our six-year-old daughter had been listening in on the conversation, strategizing on her own. When there was a break in the dialogue, our little girl looked upon us with compassion in her eyes. "Mommy and Daddy," she said, sweetly, "if you need money, you can have all of mine. I don't mind if you take it."

In that precious moment, I wasn't quite sure what to say. To be sure, even her entire life savings was a paltry sum in comparison to what we needed. Whether she was aware of that fact or not, I'm not sure she really cared. She just saw people she loved in a state of need, and she offered everything she had, hoping it would be enough.

Perhaps it is in light of that experience that I have come to so deeply treasure John 6:8-9. In his account, the response of the disciples (collectively) is actually attributed to *individuals*. It was Philip, he specifies, who exclaimed that the Master's instruction would require eight months of wages. But in bold contrast to Philip's pessimism, "Andrew, Simon Peter's brother, spoke up, 'Here is a boy with five small barley loaves and two small fish ...'" (John 6:8b-9a). Let's be honest: on its face, that was a really stupid thing to say. These men are surrounded by thousands of hungry people, and Andrew's contribution to the dilemma is to point out that, hey, we do have a little boy's snack! Maybe this will help!

I would imagine that some of the other disciples rolled their eyes. Even Andrew seems to quickly doubt the value of his own suggestion, as he goes on to concede, "but how far will they go among so many?"[13] It seemed like a worthless offering. It seemed like a pointless suggestion. And yet, those small loaves and tiny fish were precisely what the Lord used to satisfy the hunger of thousands of people that day. Imagine what He could do with the time, talents, and obedience you have to offer, if only you will put them in His hands today.

That is exactly what David did in the valley that day against the giant. As the Philistine champion bellowed out threats, while two anxious armies looked on in anticipation of a bloodbath, David's faith remained resolute:

> *"You come against me with sword and spear and javelin, but I come against you in the name of the Lord Almighty, the God of the armies of Israel, whom you have defied. This day the Lord will hand you over to me, and I'll strike you down and cut off your head. Today I will give the carcasses of the Philistine army to the birds of the air and the beasts of the earth, and the whole world will know that there is a God in Israel. All those gathered here will know that it is not by sword or spear that the Lord saves; for the battle is the Lord's, and he will give all of you into our hands." (1 Samuel 17:45-47)*

There was no hint of arrogance or pride in David's threat that day. He knew very well that he lacked the armor, the weaponry, the size and the experience necessary to win a fight. But He also knew that the battle belonged to the Lord Almighty, who was more than capable of using an ordinary kid's sling and stones to bring down a giant. Ultimately, this is the life of discipleship to which you and I are called. He's not seeking heroes. He simply invites us to offer what we have and trust that it will be enough in His hands.

Practical Action Step

If you have lived but a day in this world, you've likely encountered at least one overwhelming need. The whole world has problems, to be sure, but I want to encourage you today to look to your immediate context. Consider your neighbors, your family, your church, or your school. Whom do you see in need of compassion? Whom do you see in need of nourishment? Who is facing a dilemma that seems far bigger than you? Be reminded that the compassion of

---

[13] Gaebelein (Vol. 9), p. 72.

our Lord arrived before you ever knew about this need. Be reminded that He is responding in love to that person (or persons) already. *Now choose to offer whatever you have.* Maybe it's a gift. Maybe it's a word of encouragement. Maybe it's a talent. Or maybe it's just your time. Give it freely with the confidence that God can use what you offer to work a miracle.

As we come to the end of our journey together, I can't help but reflect again on the original invitation Jesus extended to His first disciples:

"Come, follow me, and I will make you fishers of men."

It was such a beautifully simple promise, wasn't it? The invitation was clear: *I am calling to you leave what you're doing and follow after me.* He didn't ask them to wear a Jesus t-shirt. He didn't ask them to call themselves by a particular name. He just called them to walk with Him, wherever He might go. He wanted them by His side, following His lead, doing what He did. There was no assurance of security, no guarantee of comfort ... just an invitation to jump out of the boat.

And just as his call was clear, so too was His promise: *I will make you fishers of men.* In short, I will take what you fishermen have to offer and do something amazing with your lives. With you, I will draw a broken humanity to myself.

Likewise will He do the same through you.

Therefore, go now and follow Him.

Acknowledgements

To the following loved ones I offer my sincerest thanks, for helping me bring this project to fruition:

To my amazing wife, Crissy, who graciously read these chapters in their earliest stages, giving me her most honest feedback, all while creating the time and space for me to pursue every last one of my goals. How could I even begin to express the depth of my love and admiration for you? You are the single greatest person I know, and my very best friend.

To my children, Cameron and Cailynn, who waited so patiently while I wrote every last page, rewarding me at each step of the way with hugs and play time. My life would be incomplete without you. You are, and always will be, loved.

To my professor, mentor, and friend, Matt Friedeman, without whom I never would have had the courage to write a book. I cannot thank you enough for the ways in which you have shaped me as a writer, minister, leader and man; your encouragement has meant more than you know.

To my faithful friend Juli Barker, of Martin Barker Design, who has been making my ideas look good for a great many years now. My entire family is indebted to you and yours.

To Mark Linn, Blaine Keene, and Franco Salvatori, for showing an interest in my work early on, and for your constant encouragement – not only on this project, but throughout the majority of my life.

To Mary Friedeman, Aaron Gadsby, Kent Chevalier, and Daniel Harris, for painstakingly poring over the entire manuscript, that you might pull the best effort out of me. Your loving challenges, tweaks, and pats on the back drove me to strive for excellence, while also reminding me that I was not alone in this venture.

To my church family at Trinity Chapel, who sacrificed greatly that I might pursue an education. From day one, you have loved me, embraced me, and enabled me to grow as a pastor and a teacher. I will always be grateful to God for the way in which He led us to one another.

To my parents, Dave and Terry, and to my sister, Traci, who created an environment in which I could come to know Christ as Savior. Mom, for your sacrifice; Dad, for choosing me; and Traci, for protecting me always ... I cannot thank you enough.

And of course, I offer my humble thanks and adoration to the Triune God, for making Himself known to me in new ways each day. Your word is a never-ending fountain of life; Your abiding presence is more than enough ...

And at the end of my days, my only desire is to hear Your voice inviting me home.

Made in the USA
San Bernardino, CA
19 July 2016